HEADING FOR THE SCOTTISH HILLS

Compiled by the Mountaineering Council of Scotland and the Scottish Landowners' Federation

Published by the Scottish Mountaineering Trust

First published in Great Britain in 1988 by the Scottish Mountaineering Trust

British Library Cataloguing in Publication Data.
Heading for the Scottish hills.
1. Scotland. Highlands. Hill walking - Manuals
I. Mountaineering Council of Scotland
II. Scottish Landowners Federation
796.5'22

ISBN 0-907521-24-X

Front cover: Heading up Glen Dochard towards Meall nan Eun (P. Hodgkiss)

Compilation by Maureen Prior
Maps by permission of the Ordnance Survey
Production by Peter Hodgkiss and Donald Bennet
Typesetting by Bureau-Graphics, Glasgow
Colour separations by Arneg, Glasgow
Printed by Hill and Hay, Glasgow
Bound by Hunter & Foulis, Edinburgh

For mountain safety advice please see *The Scottish Mountain Code*, compiled with the assistance of the Mountaineering Council of Scotland and published by the Scottish Sports Council

This book is published with the financial assistance of the Scottish Mountaineering Trust.

CONTENTS

CONTENTS

AREAS COVERED BY MAPS

FOREWORD

Dr Adam Watson

Despite occasional conflicts of interest there has long been a tradition of co-operation in Scotland between hill walkers and those who live and work on the land. This book should help to keep it that way.

Some visitors to the hills are against the killing of grouse or deer for sport, and others are against the owning of large estates by a few people. They are free to lobby in the hopes of getting legislative changes in future, just as those against them are free to lobby for leaving things as they are. In the meantime it is worth realising that most private estates in these days of high taxes and hard economics are businesses just as much as a factory or a petrol station. Very few owners can now afford the luxury of doing the shooting themselves, where the costs will be high and the income nil. Instead, nearly all sell the shooting, mostly to foreign clients who pay well if the quality of shooting and other services are up to the levels demanded by hard international competition.

If grouse shooting and deer shooting were banned, the only alternative land use that could provide an income for most Scottish hill landowners at the moment is intensive commercial afforestation. The open hills and moors so beloved of hill walkers and ramblers would then disappear, except for the highest unplantable land, under ploughed ground almost impossible to walk on, subsequently leading to impenetrable tracts of dense conifers. Only the forest roads would offer narrow linear access, and taking your own route at will on the hill would be a thing of the past. Hence, even if some hill walkers do not like the current system of sporting hill estates, it is in their interests to avoid the current alternative of mass intensive afforestation.

Grouse and deer shooting also provide jobs for people in parts of the country where there is very little other employment, and where a few stalkers and keepers are sometimes crucial in helping keep isolated rural schools and communities viable. If stalkers and keepers were made redundant, many remote houses in the Highlands would become derelict. Like most hill walkers, I greatly enjoy the wild places of the Highlands, where no man has ever lived, but I also remember the frequent delight of coming off the hill and seeing remote-living folk, getting a welcome cup of tea, sharing a chat with them about the hills they know so well, and often spending a comfortable night in their bothy. Something sad would happen to Scotland's many upper glens if the reekin' lum at the head of the glen, or the light in the window on a dark stormy night, were to vanish for good. And many grand individual characters would vanish too.

This booklet explains in more detail how hill walkers can help avoid disturbing deer stalking, grouse shooting and sheep farming. In this foreword I write as a hill walker, cross-country skier and mountaineer, a naturalist and conservationist, and a scientist interested in research on wildlife and land use. While a student at Aberdeen University I worked for several vacations as a deer-stalking ghillie in the Cairngorms, so I have had personal experience of the interests of both sides.

Many people go to the hill for their sport. Some want to do it by shooting at defined times of year, others by hill walking at all times of year. It is not fair that the sport of hill walking should spoil the sport of others. Nor is there any reason why walking or cross-country skiing must conflict seriously with game shooting. The estate where I worked as a ghillie was a good example, where the stalker asked hill walkers to stay off certain hills on certain days during the shooting season, but advised them of other hills where they could go without doing any harm. The walkers respected his wishes, partly because he was a great character who gave them a good bothy, hospitality, and witty conversation, but above all because he explained fair and square in simple language, why he needed their co-operation and because he suggested good alternatives. A blank, angry "No" from owners or their staff was seldom justifiable in the past, and will work no longer. But if useful information is provided and requests are put in a reasonable way, then most walkers will regard this as fair, and should criticise the few walkers who ignore the requests or even deliberately set out to disturb a day's shooting. Similarly, owners and their staff should criticise the few among their number who still act arrogantly or unreasonably towards walkers, or who try to keep people off the hill for the entire stag and hind seasons from 1st July-15th February, even though no stalking is done for much of that time. Give and take will not work unless it involves, and is seen to involve, some give on both sides.

The Scottish hills are there for all to enjoy, and for many to make a living. It is in everyone's interest to avoid conflict, and try to see the other side's point of view. The useful information provided in this publication will help ensure that co-operation is maintained to the benefit of all mountain users.

INTRODUCTION

David Hughes Hallet and Graham Little

From a loose-leafed, photocopied information sheet of a few pages in 1972, this publication has now grown into a substantial and well produced volume. The first printed version was released in 1984 and that edition provoked considerable comment and not a little criticism, something which this 1988 copy attempts to avoid. It has grown in content and we hope too, in understanding of the views of all those who live, work and enjoy themselves in the countryside.

The Scottish Landowners' Federation and the Mountaineering Council of Scotland wish to remind all those who walk and climb in the hills and mountains that there are those who earn their living in these areas and who therefore should be allowed to carry on their day-to-day work with as little disturbance as possible. This publication was first devised in answer to the criticism from hill walkers, who wished to telephone landowners before gaining access, that they had no way of finding out whom to contact. Whilst wishing to preserve the basic freedom of the hills it must be acknowledged that this freedom carries a responsibility. This responsibility in turn, carries an obligation to attempt to find out what activities are occurring and to try to avoid disrupting them. There is a reciprocal obligation upon the landowner to accept free access to the hills other than at critical times of the year.

The content of this book is clear. Essentially it provides a list of names and telephone numbers for most of the recognised hill walking areas. These can be used to make contact with people on the ground in advance of a visit. The appropriate contact for each area can be identified from the accompanying maps. These maps were a notable omission from the previous edition and we are particularly pleased that it has been possible to include them this time. It is only the kind assistance of the Scottish Mountaineering Trust, the publishers, that has made it possible to produce the book in this format.

Many people have put in a great deal of effort to collect and compile all the necessary information. Apart from the staff of the S.L.F. and members of the M.C. of S. Executive Committee, invaluable help has been received from the landowners of the properties referred to. Thanks in particular are due to Maureen Prior who has had the tedious but essential task of putting the contents together. We would also like to thank all the authors who have kindly contributed to the editorial content.

This publication is therefore very much a joint effort by the Mountaineering Council of Scotland and the Scottish Landowners' Federation. Both organisations hope that it will contribute towards a greater enjoyment and understanding of the Scottish countryside by all those who use it.

The estate boundaries shown on the maps are approximate, for area identification only, and are not intended to indicate legal accuracy.

A SUMMARY OF THE LAW RELATING TO PUBLIC ACCESS TO THE COUNTRYSIDE IN SCOTLAND

Compiled by the Scottish Landowners' Federation

The following is a factual account of the law relating to public access in Scotland. It is presented in this booklet in the belief that it is better both for the landowner and for the public, who are gaining access to land, that both should be aware of the law. This does not necessarily mean that either party should need to have recourse to the law, far less to the courts. Indeed the practice in Scotland has for many years been that the public are permitted access to the land with the acquiescence of the landowner and there have been remarkably few disputes. Most landowners are pleased to permit access, providing damage and disturbance are not caused and that walkers act in a responsible manner.

The law can best be dealt with under various headings, as follows:

(i) Pedestrian access (to include dogs)
(ii) Access by vehicle
(iii) Camping
(iv) Access with firearms

For further information see *Rights of Way: A Guide to the Law in Scotland* published by the Scottish Rights of Way Society Ltd.

(i) Pedestrian Access

In connection with access on or over private land it should be stated at the outset that 'trespass' is a term in common use but in Scotland has not been defined either by statute or, authoritatively, by Scottish courts. It can be defined shortly, however, as 'being where one has no right to be'. For example 'trespassers' would include: a person taking a short-cut through a field or a garden, a walker unaware that he is on private property, someone who believes he as a perfect right to be where he is, someone camping without permission. 'Trespass' may or may not be deliberate, it may or may not involve damage to property, and so on. A variety of circumstances can therefore give rise to a 'trespass'. There can be no objection either to those on private property, for whatever reason, with the consent of the owner or to those exercising a right of access by virtue of a public right of way, so that 'trespass' does not arise. To summarise the position, a 'trespass' is committed by a person who goes on to land owned or occupied by another without that other person's consent and without having a right to do so.

A 'trespass' having been committed, what can the person so aggrieved do about it? A simple trespass is not enshrined in statute as a 'criminal offence' so no prosecution can follow, but the owner or occupier of the property has the right either to obtain interdict (i.e. to obtain a court ruling that the trespass complained of must not occur again) against the trespasser or, if actual damage to property has been caused by the trespasser, to raise an action for damages. In addition a 'trespasser' may be asked by the owner or occupier to leave the property as quickly as possible. In the event of the trespasser refusing to leave, an owner or occupier has certain rights to force him to leave, but no greater force may be used than is reasonably necessary in the circumstances.

The pedestrian's right to take a dog on to private land is, by law, restricted to the extent that he is required to keep that dog under close control if there is a likelihood of it causing harm to stock. For example, if he were to go through a field containing sheep then the dog must either be on a lead or otherwise under the close control of the person accompanying the dog, and statutory sanctions would follow a breach of this legal requirement. Common-sense should also dictate that those exercising a legal right of access over, say, a grouse moor or deer forest, should ensure that dogs are kept under close control and not be permitted to run wild.

(ii) Access by Vehicles

This is governed both by common law and statute. You are not entitled to drive up a person's private driveway leading to his house without that person's consent, either specific or tacit, and such an action would amount to a 'trespass'. Similarly, you are not permitted access by vehicle over 'private estate or farm roads' unless you have the consent of the owner or occupier or there is a right of access (eg by virtue of a vehicular right of way). You are, of course, entitled to unrestricted access by vehicle over any public road which goes through an estate or farm.

Attention is drawn to a little known but important provision in the Road Traffic Act 1972 which requires no comment other than quoted — in Section 36 it is stated that a person commits an offence if, **without lawful authority**, he drives a motor vehicle on to any common land, moorland or other land of whatever description, not being land forming part of a road, as defined in the Roads (Scotland) Act 1984, — but note that an offence will not be constituted if the vehicle is driven on land within **15 yards of a road** for the purpose **only of parking** on that land, providing a vehicle may lawfully be driven on that road. It must be pointed out that nothing in that provision in any way affects the law of trespass to land with the resultant remedies nor, in particular, does it confer a right to park a vehicle on any land.

(iii) Camping

This is, of course, permitted on authorised sites where specific consent is given. But Section 3 of The Trespass (Scotland) Act 1865 creates the criminal offence of trespass where: 'every person who encamps on any land, being private property, without the consent or permission of the owner or legal occupier of such land, and every person who encamps or lights a fire on or near any private road or enclosed or cultivated land, or in or near any plantation, without the consent and permission of the owner or legal occupier of such a road, land or plantation, or on or near any highway, shall be guilty of an offence'. This offence is probably the nearest approach in the law of Scotland to a criminal offence of trespass itself but its extent is restricted, dealing primarily with those who 'encamp'. Under this provision there are approximately 200 prosecutions per year. Common-sense and the Litter Acts will require lawful campers to leave their camp sites tidy and free from litter, and their observance will also encourage an owner to renew permission in the future where this is sought.

(iv) Firearms

To enter onto another person's land without his consent and without reasonable excuse while carrying a firearm constitutes an offence under Section 20 of the Firearms Act 1968. You are therefore strongly recommended when out walking on another's property never to carry a firearm unless the specific permission of the owner or occupier has been obtained to do so.

There are in addition to the above, two 19th Century acts relating to poaching which create offences of trespass. The Night Poaching Act 1828 makes it an offence to enter or be on land unlawfully with instruments for taking game at night, whilst the Game (Scotland) Act 1832 makes it an offence to trespass without the leave of a proprietor 'by entering or being on during the day, land in pursuit of game or various birds'.

CONFRONTATION OR CO-OPERATION

Richard Cooke

Of the many activities that take place in the Highlands of Scotland, all compete and therefore pose a threat to the pursuit or enjoyment of each other. The present intensification of all these land uses, particularly those of a public recreational nature, inevitably increases the potential for disruption and confrontation. It is therefore incumbent on all who have an interest in the Highlands to come to an understanding of the requirements of other interests and to find a means of co-operation and co-existence.

Those who have an occupational interest — landowners, farmers, foresters, game keepers and stalkers — depend on the traditional activities of the Highlands for their livelihood and in general believe that their requirements should have priority over those whose interest is recreational — hill walkers, downhill and cross-country skiers, mountaineers, bird watchers or armed forces units on exercise. They recognise however the legitimate desire of the wider public to seek their recreation in the hills, and in some cases the influx of visitors provides opportunities to develop new business activities, which help to sustain the fragile rural economy and halt depopulation.

It is not only the estate owner who suffers when his business ceases to be viable, but also the visitor to the countryside. The quality of the landscape and wildlife which are of increasing public interest owe a great deal to the careful traditional management skills that man has evolved over many decades. If heather is not burned in rotation for grouse and sheep, it becomes rank, unattractive and less capable of supporting wildlife. If deer numbers are not controlled and kept in balance with available feeding, the inevitable result is over-population and death by starvation.

The broad consensus among landowners is to acknowledge that the Highlands are a national resource and that visitors who have taken the trouble to acquire some understanding of the Highland economy are to be welcomed. Hill walkers and others who are aware of the effect of a dog running out of control through sheep at lambing time, or of disturbing deer in heavy snow conditions when they are under stress, take the trouble to keep their distance from stock and pose no threat. Similarly those who understand that the letting of grouse shooting and deer stalking are necessary to pay the gamekeeper's wages and thus maintain consistent and constructive management, obtain the necessary local information to avoid crossing ground where these activities are taking place.

The landowners represented by the East Grampian Deer Management Group recognise the importance of promoting co-operation with hill walkers. In 1984 they erected notices throughout the East Grampian area which incorporate a guide map showing the recognised hill tracks and indicating sensitive times when public access could be damaging, recommending contact with estate staff for further directions. An information sheet has also been made available through local tourist offices and hotels. This initiative was reported in the press, on local television and radio, and was widely welcomed by members of recreational interest organisations. The East Grampian Deer Management Group entry and map in the appropriate section of this booklet is designed to complement the earlier exercise and encourage further contact between all those who have a mutual interest in maintaining the structure of the Highland economy.

In participating in the preparation of this booklet with the Mountaineering Council of Scotland, the Scottish Landowners' Federation has indicated its firm commitment to bridge the divide between resident and visitor. Hill walkers will find landowners and their employees glad to assist in pointing out a route across the hills and to explain the workings of their estate business. I would suggest that the insight gained from encounters between local people and visitors can remove at a stroke the potential for conflict and lay a foundation for long term co-existence which will enhance and protect the Highlands as we know them.

TREADING SOFTLY ON THE HILLS

Rawdon Goodier

Many years ago I found myself standing at the head of a remote valley below a great cliff renowned for its mountain plants. Instead of undisturbed alpine gardens, safeguarded from the grazing of sheep by their inaccessibility, I found a scene of devastation. At the foot of the cliff lay great piles of loose earth and stones scattered with the uprooted remains of moss campion, roseroot, saxifrages and other attractive mountain plants. I knew only too well the cause. After serving as a refuge for these plants for millenia the cliff had, within the space of a weekend, been 'developed' for rock climbing.

This experience brought home to me the paradox that arises when our 'enjoyment' of the hills is pursued to their detriment. In a less extreme way many of us who have walked the hills for years are conscious of the deterioration brought about by the simple trampling of many feet scarring the ground surface — as is often found on the most frequented routes on many Munros.

Although the actual damage done to the mountain environment by recreational use is much less in area terms than that done by bulldozed tracks and afforestation, its source in our affection for the hills makes it particularly anomalous and it tends to affect the most sensitive and most highly valued areas. While these effects may be obvious when they take the form of accelerated erosion, there may be more subtle impacts, such as the disturbance of nesting birds during the breeding season. On quite a few coastal and some inland cliffs, climbers have agreed to stay away during the breeding season of the great seabird colonies or of birds such as the peregrine. Climbers and walkers are generally aware of the need to avoid strewing litter behind them but not so good when it comes to leaving waste food in their wake, on the grounds that it is bio-degradeable. Leaving aside the remarkable longevity of banana and orange peel on Scottish summits, the food attracts scavenging species that would not normally frequent the area and these then turn to the eggs and young of more localised ground-nesting mountain birds.

There are generally very few restrictions on access to the upland national nature reserves, though where these are not owned by the Nature Conservancy Council, the owners may request the observance of codes in relation to grouse shooting and deer stalking set out elsewhere in this booklet. Reserves may, however, contain certain research or particularly sensitive areas subject to stricter rules on access. These are generally indicated on the ground by signs or markers and visitors are asked to avoid disturbing them so that the results of what may be years of research or conservation effort may be safeguarded. Similarly on some reserves fences have been erected to promote natural regeneration of woodland or other natural communities and it is vitally important that these remain sheep and deer proof, so damage to these fences should be avoided.

The exercise of access requires the cultivation of a sensitivity in our way of being in the hills, the development of a personal and shared ethic that may on occasion require a self-limitation if the hills are not to deteriorate as a result of our affection for them. It will be necessary to resist both ill-conceived projects for making access easier, particularly for vehicles, and for expanding damaging recreational activities simply to meet demand. Although some restorative measures may occasionally be possible, mountain environments do not generally lend themselves to a quick technological fix. Ultimately the best way of showing our affection for a particularly attractive area suffering from over-use may be to stay away, and persuade others to do likewise.

DON'T FOUL THE MOUNTAIN FOR YOUR FRIENDS

Tom Weir

Here is a wee story for you about that ugly subject, litter on the hills due to thoughtlessness. One keen winter day when the summit ridge of Cruachan was in fine condition for cutting steps with the axe, two of us arrived on the Dalmally peak after a fine traverse from the Taynuilt top. We'd been there a wee while, savouring the view in the windless air when coming towards us we saw three well-equipped climbers.

Retreating a little, in order to let them have the summit to themselves we heard a voice congratulating one of the trio in reaching the summit of his first Scottish Munro. At the same time we saw one peel an orange and chuck away the skin, an action promptly copied by another. At that point I walked across to them and said acidly, "I couldn't help overhearing congratulations being offered to one of your party on reaching his first Munro top. I hope it's his last if that's how your treat the mountain."

Said one, decidedly English-spoken, in public school tones, "It's organic matter. It will soon disappear." My reply was, "Meantime it's fouling the mountain for me, and your friends too if that's them I see coming along the ridge." We left them at that, but there was to be a sequel to that encounter.

Months later I happened to be in Perth when I met a man who had been a member of that bus party. He said, "You did a good job that day on Ben Cruachan. On any summit now we make sure no debris is left, for we never know when Tommy Weir may be around!" I had a good laugh too on the top of Ben Lomond where a large party of primary school children were tucking into sandwiches and swilling fruit juice. One wee lad who had sucked the last drop from his tin gave a whoop of joy as he held it high and hurled it down the hill. "What's that you are doing?' I yelled. "It's empty", he yelled back by way of explanation. Worse still, I had to retrieve the tin, since the teacher in charge thought the slope too steep and rocky for the wee boy to descend.

Carrying thirst quenching tins of drink to the tops of hills can be equated with the big rush to the hills in the 1950's, and is still accelerating. Almost any summit reveals where cans have been inserted between stones or left lying where they were drained of their contents. What goes up the mountain should be brought down; the tins that carried the drink, orange peel, banana skins, plastic bags, paper, THE LOT!

Nor is a mountainside or summit a place for plaques as memorials to climbers who have died on the mountain, or as testimony to their love of the hills. Ben Nevis has a rash of them round the ruins of the summit observatory, which has a corrugated survival hut perched on its top.

I am aware that in saying this I also include the summit indicator erected by the Scottish Mountaineering Club as a memorial to members lost in the Great War of

1914-18. This should remain because it is geographically useful in clear conditions for identifying distant peaks stretching round in every direction. The historic observatory ruin should remain too. And what an improvement it would be if the present corrugated survival hut could be replaced by a stone-built structure to be used only in emergency.

My plea to all who go to the mountains is to leave them as clean as you find them, or cleaner if you carry some unsightly debris down. The little verse below says it all, I don't know who wrote it:

Let not one say,
And say it to my shame,
That all was beauty there,
Until I came.

What goes for the tops goes for the glens, the footpaths and the bothies. We must try to make unthinking people think. In Britain we have to face the fact that we are not a clean nation. The sudden popularity of the hills in the post-war period testifies to the fact. So let's reverse that fact and try to keep the places we love clean.

THE PROFESSIONAL APPROACH

Mick Tighe (NEVIS GUIDES)

As full-time Mountain Guides, working for the most part in Scotland, we make our living on other people's property; our access requirements may therefore be described as fairly unique, as our livelihood could well be at stake if we don't get it right. Perhaps a good way to describe our collective relationship with the various landowners would be as a marriage, something to be worked at in order to attain peace, harmony and ultimate satisfaction!

Though the lairds themselves may need a collective wooing, it's often the keepers and ghillies to whom we must direct our courting intentions as they are the ones most frequently encountered on the hill, and sometimes in the bar(!), and though the 'highheidiuns' may not like it, they are the people who really know what's afoot. Many of these bewhiskered 'foreandafters' become friends and relationships blossom. We get to take a few liberties on their backyard, and in return keep them informed as to what's 'moving' on the hill, and maybe indicate if anyone is taking unnecessary liberties themselves. The 'fair maiden' must be careful though, not to deny the rustic swain access to her treasures. She may wish to demur for a month or two each year to get the household affairs in order and no potential suitor could logically deny her this sabbatical. Continuous denial though, can only lead to frustration and eventually, confrontation.

The reader of this booklet may not yearn for such a deep relationship as the one portrayed above, so for the weekend walker, summer holidaymaker or group leader looking for access to the mountains, a little flirting may be the answer, and this booklet is designed to increase your potential conquests without fear of rejection. So seek out the object of your desires, do your homework; write, phone, visit, speak, understand, learn and hopefully you'll gain the key (perhaps literally) to the greater pleasures beyond.

THE FOUR R'S

Roger Smith

Since coming to live and work in Scotland ten years ago, my greatest pleasure has been to wander the hills of this, my adopted country. The greatest part of that pleasure has been the freedom to wander where I choose, whether for a half-day on the Ochils or a two-week backpack right across the country.

That freedom is very precious: it releases us from narrowly defined footpaths, those soulless access corridors found elsewhere in these islands, and it must be maintained and defended with all the vigour at our command. It is a freedom from rules, regulations and restrictions, three of my four R's.

We do not need those three, but to ensure that happy situation continues, we must ourselves put in place the fourth R: responsibility of behaviour. It is not much to ask that for a small part of the year — mid-August to mid-October — we respect to the full the requirements of estates with regard to stalking for sport. I personally greatly regret that the income from this activity is so vital to Highland estates, but while it is, we have no right to jeopardise that income by thoughtless action.

In return, it is not much to ask of estates that they leave us be for the rest of the year. The true stravaiger in Scotland treads quietly and does not disturb land or wildlife with his passing. He contributes to the local economy whenever he can and if he is left to pursue his pleasure in peace, he will return. I look forward to many more years of wandering the hills of Scotland, and when I am too decrepit to climb the hills, I shall still wander the glens. It is a continual learning process, and I see no reason whatever for what I do to conflict in any way with the rightful activity of those who own and work the land, or as I would prefer to put it, have the land in their stewardship. We are all guardians, and we must ensure that we pass on to future generations both a countryside they can be proud to enjoy, and the priceless freedom to enjoy it.

Roger Smith is editor of the magazine *Environment Now*, and has associations with a number of conservation bodies in Scotland. The views he expresses here are however entirely his own.

THE FORESTRY COMMISSION VIEW

The Commission welcomes the public on foot to all its forests, provided this access does not conflict with the management and protection of the forest, and provided there are no legal agreements which would be infringed by unrestricted public access.

The main emphasis is in the provision of facilities for day visitors, providing car parks, picnic places, viewpoints and forest walks, particularly where they are readily accessible to visitors from towns and holiday centres. Information and interpretation about the forests and surrounding countryside are provided in order to help visitors to appreciate them better.

Access on foot to all its forests is free of charge. However, for centres established to provide information and interpretation (Visitor Centres), for car parks and other facilities a charge may be made where its collection is feasible.

The Commission has constructed thousands of miles of forest roads in Scotland for the efficient harvesting of timber and the management and protection of the forest. These roads also provide access to many beautiful and remote areas. Although the Commission believes this access should be for those on foot, a very small number of forest roads are used additionally as 'forest drives'.

The regular use of forest by motor vehicles for recreational purposes is prohibited except where it is necessary for access to particular facilities, for example car parks, picnic places, and camping sites, within the forest.

A limited number or 'forest drives' consisting of specially designated forest roads through scenic parts of the forest, are operated as toll roads.

A leaflet describing the Commission's Forest Parks, where a wide range of recreation facilities are provided, is available from Public Information Division, 231 Corstorphine Road, Edinburgh EH12 7AT (telephone 031 334 0303).

Follow the Forest Code:

1. Guard against all risk of **fire**
2. **Protect** trees, plants and wildlife
3. **Leave things** as you find them. Take nothing away
4. **Keep dogs** and animals under proper control
5. **Avoid** damaging buildings, fences, hedges, walls and signs
6. **Leave** no litter
7. **Respect** the work of the forest. Observe all signs; do not leave open or obstruct gates; for your own safety keep clear of forestry operations
8. Do not carry **firearms or weapons** of any kind
9. **Camp** only on approved camp sites
10. Remember that **vehicles** are not allowed except by arrangement
11. Obtain **permits** for horse riding, fishing and other special activities, if in doubt ask at the forest office
12. **Respect** the peace and quiet of the forest and avoid disturbing others

IMPORTANT TIMES OF THE YEAR FOR SOME COUNTRYSIDE ACTIVITIES

Red Deer Stalking: the open season for culling red deer stags is from 1st July - 20th October, and for hinds from 21st October - 15th February. However, the most critical time is generally from mid-August to mid-October.

Lambing: the exact time of hill lambing in Scotland varies according to the area, but is generally between mid-April and the end of May.

Grouse Shooting: the grouse shooting season runs from the 12th August to 10th December, with most shoots taking place during the earlier part of that period

Ground nesting birds on moorland can be very vulnerable to disturbance, and walkers will therefore wish to take particular care at nesting time.

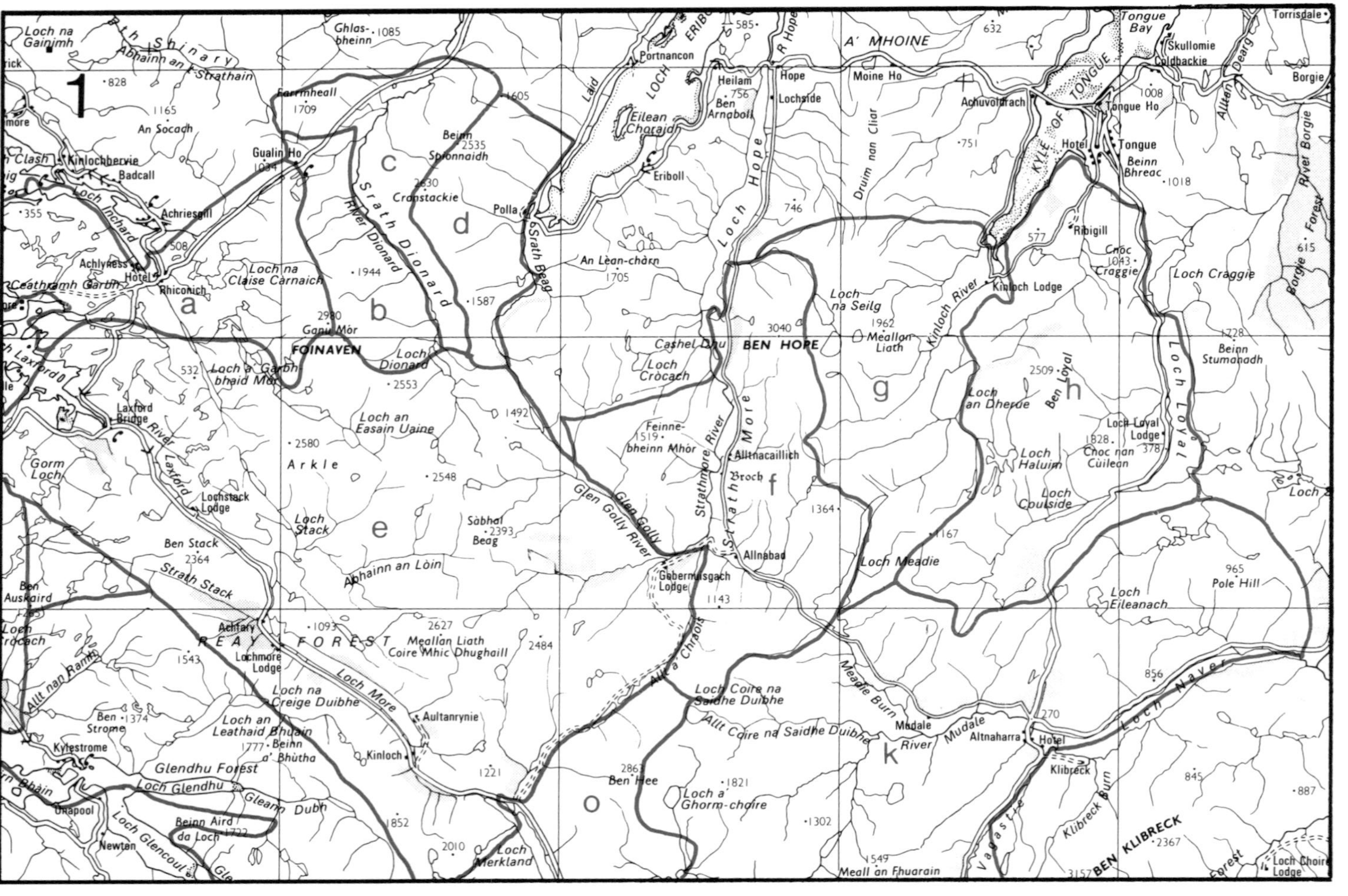

1
BEN HOPE
FOINAVEN
BEN KLIBRECK
A' MHOINE
KYLE OF TONGUE
LOCH ERIBOLL
REAY FOREST
Ben Loyal
Ben Hee
Ben Stack
Arkle
Loch Loyal
Loch Hope
Loch Stack
Loch More
Loch Naver
Loch Inchard
Loch Meadie
Loch Craggie
Strath Dionard
Strath Stack
Strath Beag
Strathmore River
Glen Golly
Glen Golly River
Kinloch River
River Laxford
River Mudale
Tongue
Tongue Bay
Hope
Heilam
Eriboll
Portnancon
Kinlochbervie
Rhiconich
Achfary
Altnaharra
Kylestrome
Unapool
Pole Hill
Beinn Stumanadh
Meallan Liath
Cranstackie
Beinn Spionnaidh
Farrmheall

Map 1 — Reay Forest — Ben Hope

Reference	Estate Name
1a	RHICONICH
1b	GUALIN HOUSE
1c	BALNAKEIL
1d	RISPOND & POLLA
1e	REAY FOREST
1f	STRATHMORE
1g	KINLOCH
1h	BEN LOYAL
1k	ALTNAHARRA
1o	MERKLAND

Hills

Cranstackie
Beinn Spionnaidh
Foinaven
Arkle
Ben Stack
Ben Hope
Ben Loyal
Ben Hee

Map/Estate Reference	Mountain or Mountain Group	Approaches	Estate	Contact	Remarks
1d	Cranstackie and Beinn Spionnaidh	From east (Loch Eriboll)	RISPOND & POLLA Mr. & Mrs. C. Marsham Rispond, Durness by Lairg Sutherland	Mr. & Mrs. C. Marsham Rispond Durness Tel: Durness (097 181) 224	No parking available at Polla Cottage.
1c		From west	BALNAKEIL Messrs Elliot Balnakeil House Balnakeil, Durness by Lairg, Sutherland	General Manager Peter C. Anderson Tel: Durness (097 181) 268	Dogs off leash not welcome. Please contact at lambing time and stag stalking season.
1e	Foinaven, Arkle and Ben Stack	Via existing footpaths	REAY FOREST Trustees of 2nd Duke of Westminster per S.C. Mackintosh Estate Office Achfary, by Lairg Sutherland	Estate Office Achfary, by Lairg Sutherland Tel: Lochmore (097 184) 221	
1b		From north	GUALIN HOUSE Mr Pat Wilson Loanleven, Almondbank, Perth. PH1 3NF		

1a		From north-west	RHICONICH Mr Richard Osborne Sandyland House, Runnington Wellington, Somerset, TA21 02N		
1f	Ben Hope	From south-west	STRATHMORE Mrs D.J.H. Gow Pitscandly, Forfar Angus	The Stalker Strathmore Altnaharra Tel: Altnaharra (054 981) 248	Please park in lay-by and not at the cattle shed.
1g		From east	KINLOCH A.W.G. Sykes Kinloch Lodge Tongue, Sutherland	A. Henderson The Stalker Tel: Tongue (084 755) 316	Parking only available on public highway.
1h	Ben Loyal	From north-east	BEN LOYAL Lt. Col. J.G. Moncrieff Loch Loyal Lodge Lairg, Sutherland, IV27 4AF	Loch Loyal Lodge Lairg, Sutherland Tel: Tongue (084 755) 291 or 220	
1k		From south	ALTNAHARRA North Clebrig Farms Ltd Altnaharra Lodge Lairg, Sutherland IV27 4AE	Alistair MacDonald Head Keeper Lairg, Sutherland Tel: Altnaharra (054 981) 220	

Map/Estate Reference	Mountain or Mountain Group	Approaches	Estate	Contact	Remarks
1g		From west	KINLOCH A.W.G. Sykes Kinloch Lodge Tongue, Sutherland	A.Henderson The Stalker Tel: Tongue (084 755) 316	Parking only available on public highway.
1k	Ben Hee	From east	ALTNAHARRA North Clebrig Farms Ltd Altnaharra Lodge Lairg Sutherland IV27 4AE	Alistair MacDonald Head Keeper Altnaharra Lairg, Sutherland Tel: Altnaharra (054 981) 220	
1o		From south	MERKLAND Mr Robert Woods The Old Rectory Frilsham, Nr Newbury Berkshire RG16 9XH	Mr Alan Walker Stalker Tel: Merkland (054 983) 222	
1e		From north-west	REAY FOREST Trustees of 2nd Duke of Westminster per S.C. Mackintosh Estate Office, Achfary by Lairg, Sutherland	Estate Office Achfary, by Lairg Sutherland Tel: Lochmore (097 184) 221	

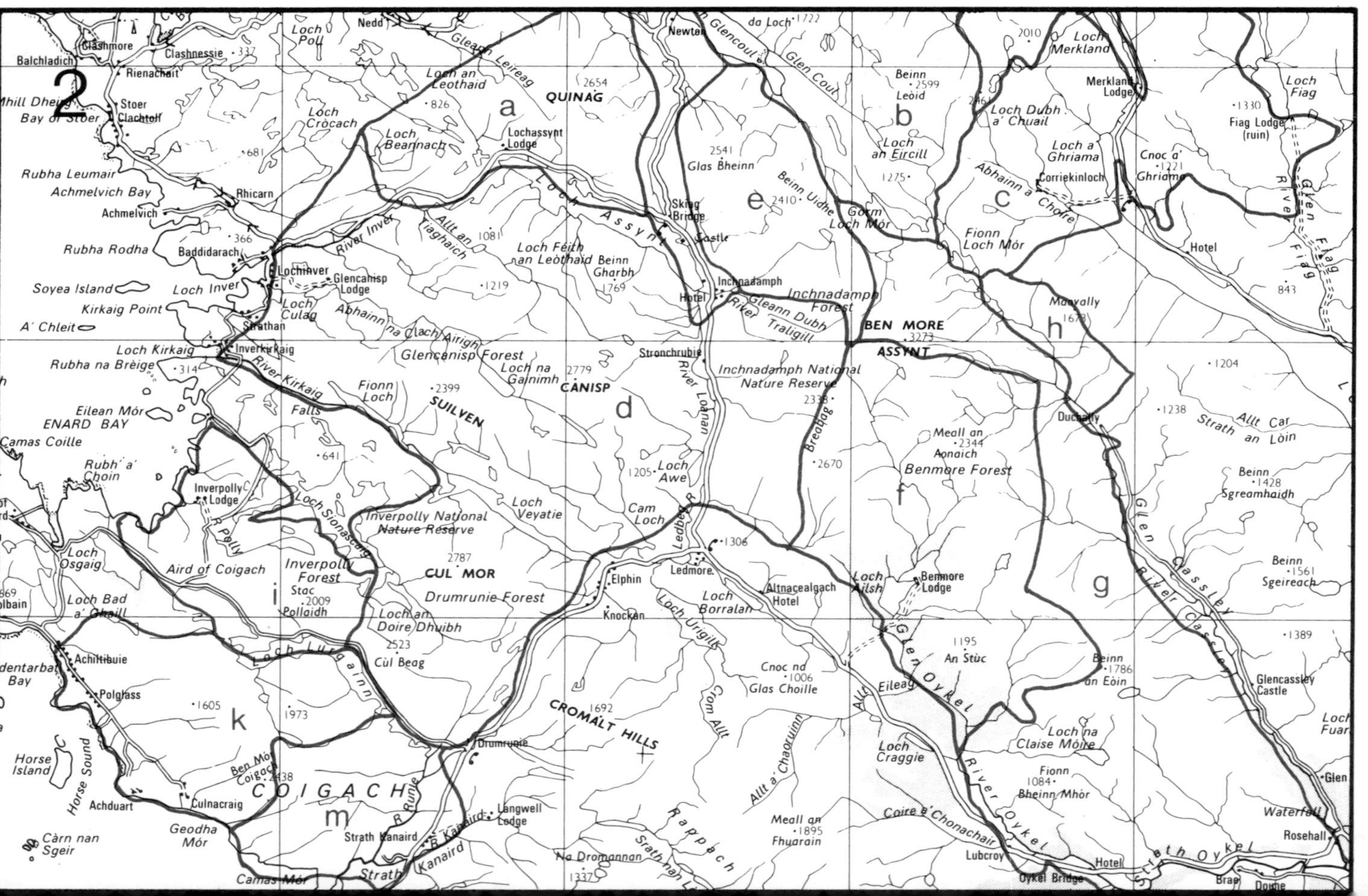

2
Balchladich
Clashmore
Clashnessie
337
Rienachait
Stoer
Clachtoll
Bay of Stoer
681
Rubha Leumair
Achmelvich Bay
Achmelvich
Rhicarn
366
Rubha Rodha
Baddidarach
Soyea Island
Loch Inver
Kirkaig Point
A' Chleit
Loch Kirkaig
Rubha na Brèige
314
Eilean Mór
ENARD BAY
Camas Coille
Rubh' a' Choin
Loch Osgaig
Loch Bad a' Ghaill
Achiltibuie
Polglass
Horse Island
Horse Sound
Achduart
Culnacraig
Geodha Mór
Càrn nan Sgeir
Camas Mór
Loch Poll
Nedd
Gleann Leireag
Loch an Leothaid
826
Loch Cròcach
Loch Beannach
a
QUINAG
2654
Lochassynt Lodge
Loch Assynt
River Inver
Allt an Tiaghaich
1081
Loch Fèith an Leòthaid
Beinn Gharbh
1769
Lochinver
Glencanisp Lodge
Loch Culag
Strathan
1219
Abhainn na Clach Airigh
Inverkirkaig
River Kirkaig
Glencanisp Forest
Loch na Gainimh
2779
CANISP
Fionn Loch
2399
SUILVEN
Falls
641
d
Inverpolly Lodge
R. Polly
Loch Sionascaig
Inverpolly National Nature Reserve
Loch Veyatie
Aird of Coigach
Inverpolly Forest
2787
CUL MOR
Drumrunie Forest
i
Stac Pollaidh
2009
Loch an Doire Dhuibh
2523
Cùl Beag
Loch Lurgainn
1605
k
1973
Ben Mór Coigach
2438
COIGACH
m
R. Runie
Strath Kanaird
R. Kanaird
Langwell Lodge
Drumrunie
Newton
Glencoul
da Loch
1722
Glen Coul
2541
Glas Bheinn
e
2410
Beinn Uidhe
Skiag Bridge
Castle
Inchnadamph
Hotel
Gleann Dubh
River Traligill
Inchnadamph Forest
Stronchrubie
River Loanan
Inchnadamph National Nature Reserve
2338
Breabag
2670
1205
Loch Awe
Cam Loch
Ledbeg R.
1306
Elphin
Ledmore
Knockan
Loch Borralan
Loch Urigill
Altnacealgach Hotel
Cnoc na Glas Choille
1006
Crom Allt
1692
CROMALT HILLS
Allt a' Chaoruinn
Rappach
Strath nan L
Na Dromannan
1337
Meall an Fhuarain
1895
Beinn Leòid
2599
b
Loch an Eircill
1275
Gorm Loch Mór
BEN MORE ASSYNT
3273
Meall an Aonaich
2344
Benmore Forest
f
Loch Ailsh
Benmore Lodge
Glen Oykel
Allt Eileag
Loch Craggie
1195
An Stùc
Coire a' Chonachair
River Oykel
Lubcroy
Oykel Bridge
2010
Loch Merkland
Merkland Lodge
Loch Dubh a' Chuail
Loch a Ghriama
Corriekinloch
Abhainn a Choire
c
Fionn Loch Mór
Meavally
1678
h
Duchally
g
Beinn an Eòin
1786
Loch na Claise Mòire
Fionn Bheinn Mhòr
1084
Hotel
Strath Oykel
Loch Fiag
1330
Fiag Lodge (ruin)
Cnoc a' Ghriama
1221
Glen Fiag
River Fiag
Hotel
843
1204
1238
Strath an Lòin
Allt Car
Beinn Sgreamhaidh
1428
Glen Cassley
River Cassley
Beinn Sgeireach
1561
1389
Glencassley Castle
Loch Fuar
Glen
Waterfall
Rosehall
Brae
Doune

Map 2 — Assynt — Coigach

Reference	Estate Name
2a	LOCH ASSYNT ESTATE
2b	KYLESTROME
2c	MERKLAND
2d	GLENCANISP AND DRUMRUNIE
2e	INCHNADAMPH
2f	BEN MORE
2g	INVERCASSELEY
2h	DUCHALLY
2i	INVERPOLLY
2k	BEN MORE COIGACH
2m	KEANCHULISH

Hills

Quinag
Suilven
Canisp
Ben More Assynt
Conival

Cul Mor
Cul Beag
Stac Pollaidh
Ben More Coigach

Map/Estate Reference	Mountain or Mountain Group	Approaches	Estate	Contact	Remarks
2a	Quinag	Via existing paths	LOCH ASSYNT ESTATE Mrs W. Filmer-Sankey Loch Assynt Lodge By Lairg, Sutherland	Mrs W. Filmer-Sankey Loch Assynt Lodge Tel: Assynt (057 12) 216	Good car park beyond Shepherd's cottage and access gate opposite
2d	Suilven and Canisp	From west - Lochinver and Suileag	GLENCANISP AND DRUMRUNIE DEER FOREST TRUST Trustees of Trust Lochinver Estate Office Lochinver, Sutherland	Lochniver Estate Office, Lochinver Tel: Lochinver (057 14) 203	Leaflet available from Estate Office.
2e	Ben More Assynt and Conival	From west - Inchnadamph approach via Gleann Dubh	INCHNADAMPH Assynt Trading Co. Ltd Lochinver Estate Office Lochinver Sutherland	The Keeper Tel: Assynt (057 12) 221 or Tel: Lochinver (057 14) 203	Please park on main road.
2f		From south - Loch Ailsh and Glen Oykel	BEN MORE Assynt Trading Co. Ltd. Lochinver Estate Office Lochinver Sutherland	The Keeper Tel: Elphin (085 484) 235 or Lochinver Estate Office Tel: Lochinver (057 14) 203	Please park beside notice at south end of Loch Ailsh

2b		From north	KYLESTROME Lady Mary Grosvenor Kylestrome Lodge, Kylesku Lairg, Sutherland, IV27 4TL		
2c		From north-east	MERKLAND Mr Robert Woods The Old Rectory Frilsham, Nr Newbury Berks RG16 9XH	Mr Alan Walker Stalker Tel: Merkland (054 983) 222	
2h		From east	DUCHALLY Balmagown Castle Property Ltd Balmagown Kildary, Ross-shire, IV18 0NU		
2g			INVERCASSELEY Mrs D Dowdeswell Lower Radbourne Farm Southam, Lemington Spa Warwickshire CU33 0NH		
2d	Cul Mor and Cul Beag	From east	GLENCANISP AND DRUMRUNIE DEER FOREST TRUST Trustees of Trust Lochinver Estate Office Lochinver, Sutherland	The Keeper Tel: Elphin (085 484) 238 or Lochinver Estate Office Tel: Lochinver (057 14) 203	Please park on main road. Leaflet available from Estate Office

Map/Estate Reference	Mountain or Mountain Group	Approaches	Estate	Contact	Remarks
2i		From west	INVERPOLLY Rt. Hon E. Davies Inverpolly Lodge Lochinver, Sutherland	Mr C. MacDonald Ardnahaird Tel: Lochinver (057 14) 252	
2i	Stac Pollaidh	From south, Loch Lurgainn	INVERPOLLY (as above)	Mr C. MacDonald Ardnahaird Tel: Lochinver (057 14) 252	
2d		From east	GLENCANISP DRUMRUNIE DEER FOREST TRUST Trustees of Trust Lochinver Estate Office Lochinver, Sutherland	The Keeper Tel: Elphin (085 484) 238 or Lochinver Estate Office Tel: Lochinver (057 14) 203	Please park on main road. Leaflet available from Estate Office.
2k	Ben More Coigach	From north-west Achiltibuie	BEN MORE COIGACH Scottish Wildlife Trust c/o Finlayson Hughes 45 Church Street Inverness IV1 1DR	Ground Warden I. Campbell 132 Polglass Achiltibuie Tel: Achiltibuie (085 482) 363	Car park at Culnacraig. Contact Wildlife Warden for information during summer months.

2m	From south-east Strath Kanaird	KEANCHULISH Mr. L. Bramall Runie Lodge Strathcanaird Ullapool	Not required	Car park at Blughasary. Lay-by on the west side of the main road between Stathkanaird and Drumrunie phone box

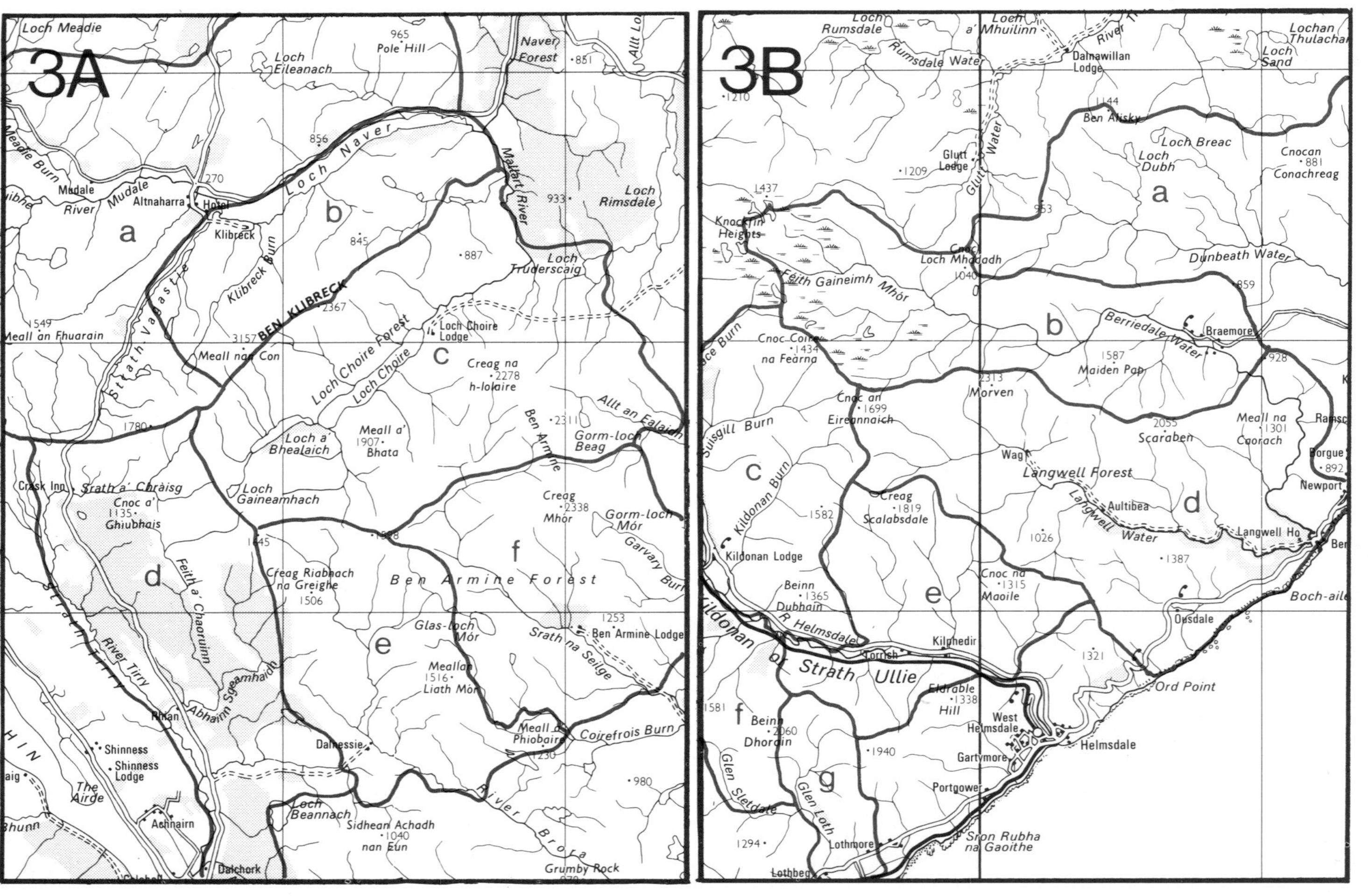

3A
Loch Meadie
Meadie Burn
Mudale
River
Mudale
Altnaharra
Hotel
270
Klibreck
Klibreck Burn
Loch Naver
Loch Eileanach
Pole Hill
965
856
845
887
Naver Forest
851
Mallart River
933
Loch Rimsdale
Loch Truderscaig
BEN KLIBRECK
2367
3157
Meall nan Con
1549
Meall an Fhuarain
Strath Vagastie
1780
Loch Choire Lodge
Loch Choire Forest
Loch Choire
Creag na h-Iolaire
2278
Ben Armine
2311
Allt an Ealaich
Gorm-loch Beag
Gorm-loch Mór
Garvary Burn
Creag Mhór
2338
Ben Armine Forest
Ben Armine Lodge
1253
Srath na Seilge
Coirefrois Burn
980
Meall a' Bhata
1907
Loch a' Bhealaich
Loch Gaineamhach
Creag Riabhach na Greighe
1506
1645
Glas-loch Mór
Meallan Liath Mór
1516
Meall a' Phiobaire
1230
Sidhean Achadh nan Eun
1040
Loch Beannach
Dalnessie
Abhainn Sgeamhaidh
Feith a' Chaoruinn
Crask Inn
Strath a' Chràisg
Cnoc a' Ghiubhais
1135
Strath Tirry
River Tirry
Rhian
Shinness
Shinness Lodge
The Airde
Achnairn
Dalchork
River Brora
Grumby Rock
3B
Loch Rumsdale
Rumsdale Water
Loch a' Mhuilinn
Dalnawillan Lodge
Lochan Thulachan
Loch Sand
1210
1144
Ben Alisky
Loch Breac
Loch Dubh
Cnocan Conachreag
881
Glutt Lodge
Glutt Water
1209
1437
Knockfin Heights
953
Cnoc Loch Mhadadh
1040
Dunbeath Water
859
Feith Gaineimh Mhór
Braemore
Berriedale Water
928
Cnoc Coire na Fearna
1434
Maiden Pap
1587
Morven
2313
Cnoc an Eireannaich
1699
Suisgill Burn
2055
Scaraben
Meall na Caorach
1301
Borgue
892
Newport
Wag
Langwell Forest
Aultibea
Langwell Water
Langwell Ho
Kildonan Burn
1582
Creag Scalabsdale
1819
1026
1387
Kildonan Lodge
Beinn Dubhain
1365
Cnoc na Maoile
1315
Boch-aile
Ousdale
R. Helmsdale
Kilphedir
Torrish
Kildonan or Strath Ullie
1321
Ord Point
Eldrable Hill
1338
West Helmsdale
Helmsdale
1581
Beinn Dhorain
2060
1940
Gartymore
Portgower
Glen Sletdale
Glen Loth
1294
Lothmore
Sron Rubha na Gaoithe
Lothbeg

Map 3A — Klibreck

Reference	Estate Name
3A/a	ALTNAHARRA
3A/b	CLEBRIG
3A/c	LOCH CHOIRE ESTATE
3A/d	WEST SHINESS
3A/e	DALNESSIE
3A/f	BEN ARMINE

Hills

Ben Klibreck
Creag Mhor

Map 3B — Morven

Reference	Estate Name
3B/a	DUNBEATH
3B/b	BREAMORE
3B/c	SUISGILL
3B/d	LANGWELL
3B/e	TORRISH
3B/f	KILDONAN
3B/g	CRAKAIG

Hills

Morven
Scaraben
Beinn Dhorain

Map/Estate Reference	Mountain or Mountain Group	Approaches	Estate	Contact	Remarks
3A/a	Ben Klibreck	From west (A 836 between Altnaharra and Crask Inn)	ALTNAHARRA North Clebrig Farms Ltd. Altnaharra Lodge Lairg, Sutherland IV27 4AE	Alistair MacDonald Head Keeper, Altnaharra Lairg, Sutherland Tel: Altnaharra (054 981) 220	Car park by Vagastie Bridge
3A/b		From west and north	CLEBRIG Mrs. J. Nicholson Clebrig Altnaharra Lairg, Sutherland IV27 4VQ	D.G. MacKay Manager Clebrig, Altnaharra Lairg, Sutherland Tel: Altnaharra (054 981) 251	
3A/c		From east and south	LOCH CHOIRE ESTATE Lord Joicey and Mr D.A. Knowles Loch Choire Lodge, Kinbrace Sutherland KW11 6UD	A.J. Grant Loch Choire Kinbrace, Sutherland Tel: Kinbrace (043 13) 222	
3A/d		From south-west	WEST SHINNESS Mrs Parrott The Crofthouse West Shinness by Lairg, Sutherland		

3A/c	Creag Mhor	From north	LOCH CHOIRE ESTATE Lord Joicey and Mr D.A. Knowles Loch Choire Lodge, Kinbrace Sutherland KW11 6UD	A.J.Grant Loch Choire Kinbrace, Sutherland Tel: Kinbrace (043 13) 222	
3A/f		From south	BEN ARMINE Lord Strathnaver Sutherland Estates Office Golspie, Sutherland KW10 0RR	Sutherland Estates Office Tel: Golspie (040 83) 3268	
3A/e		From south-west	DALNESSIE Prof. Smillie per Arthur Young Chartered Surveyors Manor Street, Forfar DD8 1EX	The Keeper Ian Hepburn Tel: Lairg (0549) 2435	
3A/d		From west	WEST SHINNESS Mrs Parrott The Crofthouse, West Shinness by Lairg, Sutherland		
3B/b	Morven and Scaraben	All approaches	BRAEMORE The Welbeck Estates Co. Ltd Portand Estate Office Berriedale, Caithness KW7 6HE	J. Miller Braemore Keeper Braemore, Dunbeath Tel: Dunbeath (059 33) 371	Please park by public call box at Braemore.

Map/Estate Reference	Mountain or Mountain Group	Approaches	Estate	Contact	Remarks
3B/d			LANGWELL The Welbeck Estates Co. Ltd. Portland Estate Office Berriedale Caithness KW7 6HE	J.Miller Braemore Keeper Keeper's House, Braemore Tel: Dunbeath (059 33) 371	Please park by public call box at Braemore
3B/a		From north	SUISGILL Mr E.M. Reeves Suisgill Estate, Kilodonan Helmsdale, Sutherland KW8 6HY		
3B/f	Beinn Dhorain	From Strath Ullie	KILDONAN Mrs M.E.A. Clay Kildonan Lodge, Helmsdale Sutherland KW8 6HY	Head Keeper Tel: Kinbrace (043 13) 263	
3B/e		From north-east	TORRISH Torrish Estate Co. Ltd. Torrish, Helmsdale Sutherland		
3B/g	Beinn Dhorain	From east	CRAKAIG Mrs. M. Dudgeon Crakaig Loch Helmsdale Sutherland		

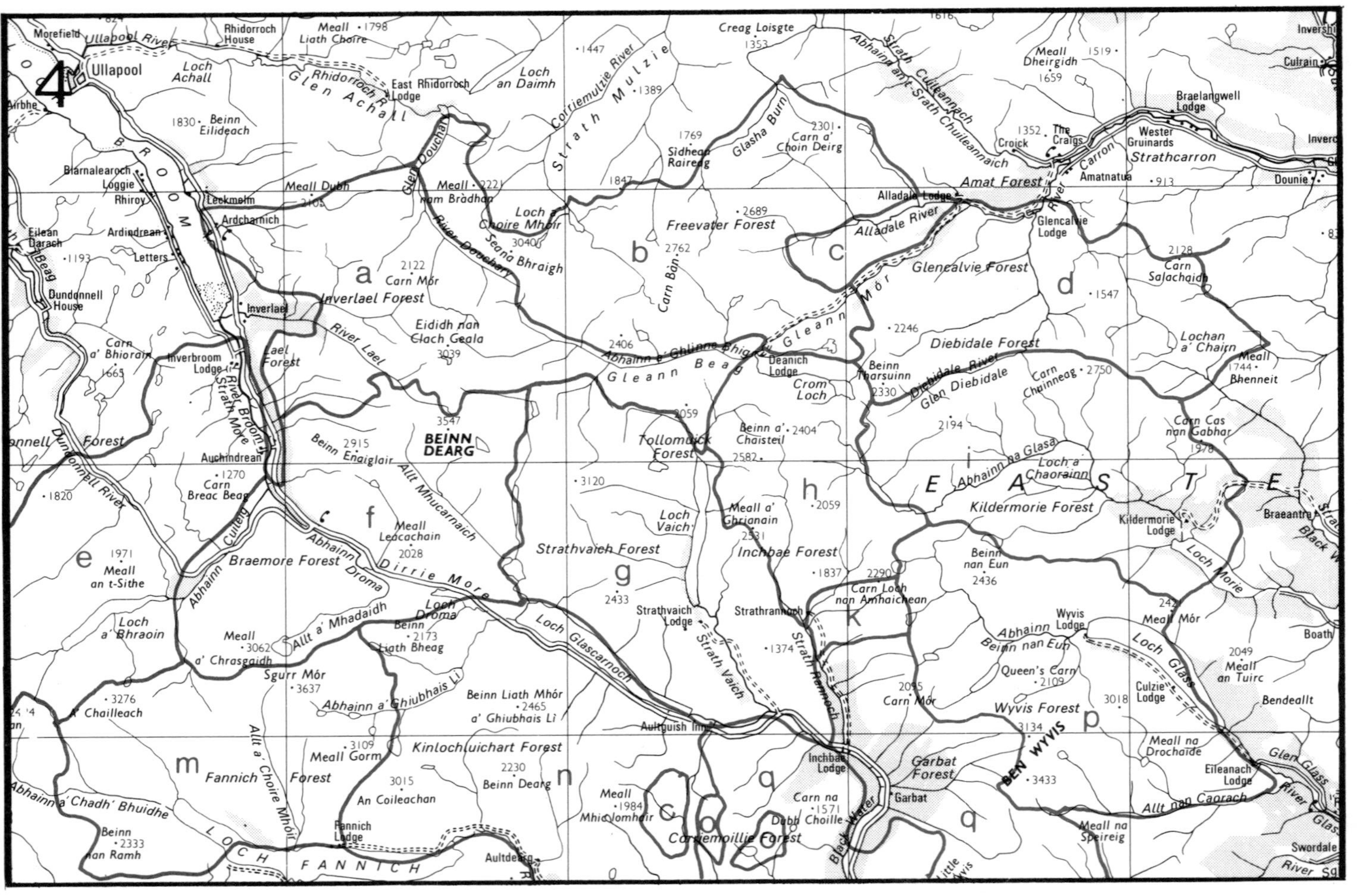

4
Ullapool
Morefield
Ullapool River
Loch Achall
Rhidorroch House
Meall Liath Choire
Rhidorroch
Glen Achall
East Rhidorroch Lodge
Loch an Daimh
Corriemulzie River
Strath Mulzie
Creag Loisgte
Glasha Burn
Carn a' Choin Deirg
Sidhean Rairelg
Strath Cuileannach
Abhainn an t-Strath Chuileannach
Meall Dheirgidh
Croick
The Craigs
Carron
Amatnatua
Strathcarron
Wester Gruinards
Braelangwell Lodge
Culrain
Dounie
Beinn Eilideach
BROOM
Blarnalearoch
Loggie
Rhiroy
Leckmelm
Ardcharnich
Ardindrean
Letters
Eilean Darach
Dundonnell House
Meall Dubh
Glen Douchary
Meall nam Bràdhan
River Douchary
Loch a' Choire Mhòir
Seana Bhraigh
Freevater Forest
Carn Bàn
Alladale Lodge
Alladale River
Amat Forest
Glencalvie Lodge
Glencalvie Forest
Carn Salachaidh
Lochan a' Chairn
Meall Bhenneit
Carn Mòr
Inverlael Forest
Inverlael
Eididh nan Clach Geala
River Lael
Lael Forest
Abhainn a' Ghlinne Bhig
Gleann Mòr
Gleann Beag
Deanich Lodge
Crom Loch
Beinn Tharsuinn
Diebidale Forest
Diebidale River
Glen Diebidale
Carn Chuinneag
Carn Cas nan Gabhar
Carn a' Bhiorain
Inverbroom Lodge
River Broom
Strath More
Dundonnell Forest
Dundonnell River
Auchindrean
Carn Breac Beag
BEINN DEARG
Beinn Enaiglair
Allt Mhucarnaich
Tollomuick Forest
Beinn a' Chaisteil
Abhainn na Glasa
Loch a' Chaorainn
EASTER
Kildermorie Forest
Kildermorie Lodge
Loch Morie
Braeantra
Black Water
Meall Leacachain
Abhainn Droma
Braemore Forest
Abhainn Cuileig
Dirrie More
Loch Vaich
Meall a' Ghrianain
Inchbae Forest
Strathvaich Forest
Meall an t-Sithe
Loch a' Bhraoin
Meall a' Chrasgaidh
Allt a' Mhadaidh
Loch Droma
Beinn Liath Bheag
Loch Glascarnoch
Strathvaich Lodge
Strath Vaich
Strathrannoch
Strath Rannoch
Carn Loch nan Amhaichean
Beinn nan Eun
Wyvis Lodge
Abhainn Beinn nan Eun
Loch Glass
Meall Mór
Boath
Meall an Tuirc
Bendeallt
Sgurr Mór
Abhainn a' Ghiubhais Li
Beinn Liath Mhór a' Ghiubhais Li
Carn Mòr
Queen's Carn
Culzie Lodge
Wyvis Forest
BEN WYVIS
Meall na Drochaide
Eileanach Lodge
Glen Glass
River Glass
A' Chailleach
Allt a' Choire Mhóir
Meall Gorm
Kinlochluichart Forest
Aultguish Inn
Inchbae Lodge
Garbat Forest
Garbat
Fannich Forest
An Coileachan
Beinn Dearg
Meall Mhic Iomhair
Carn na Dubh Choille
Corriemoillie Forest
Allt nan Caorach
Meall na Speireig
Swordale
Abhainn a' Chadh' Bhuidhe
Beinn nan Ramh
LOCH FANNICH
Fannich Lodge
Aultdearg

Map 4 — Loch Broom — Ben Wyvis

Reference	Estate Name
4a	INVERLAEL
4b	DEANICH
4c	GLENMORE
4d	GLENCALVIE
4e	INVERBROOM
4f	BRAEMORE
4g	STRATHVAICH
4h	STRATH RANNOCH
4i	KILDERMORIE
4k	INCHBAE
4m	FANNICH
4n	LOCHLUICHART
4o	CORRIEMOILLIE
4p	WYVIS
4q	FORESTRY COMMISSION

Hills

Beinn Dearg Group
Beinn a' Chaisteil
Beinn Tharsuinn
Western Fannichs
Eastern Fannichs
Corriemoillie Forest
Ben Wyvis

Map/Estate Reference	Mountain or Mountain Group	Approaches	Estate	Contact	Remarks
4a	Beinn Dearg Group	Via Gleann na Sguaib	INVERLAEL Dr S.M. Whitterridge Inverlael, Lochbroom IV23 2RG	Duncan Cameron Inverlael Farm Lochbroom Tel: Lochbroom (085 485) 262	
4f		Dirrie More	BRAEMORE Mr Stokes-Rees 86 Westbourne Park Road London W2 5PL	The Keeper Tel: Lochbroom (085 485) 222	
4g		From south	STRATHVAICH Strathvaich Partners Strathvaich Lodge Ross-shire	Ian Bennett The Keeper Tel: Aultguish (099 75) 226	
4b		From north-east	DEANICH Richard Macaire per Roderick Noble Finlayson Hughes Estate Office Ardgay, Sutherland	Finlayson Hughes Estate Office Ardgay Tel: Ardgay (086 32) 553	
4h	Beinn a' Chaisteil Beinn Tharsuinn	All apporaches	STRATH RANNOCH Strathvaich Partners Strathvaich Lodge Ross-shire	The Keeper Tel: Aultguish (099 75) 230	Parking on A835.

4i		From south-east	KILDERMORIE Capt. A.D. Hignett Kildermorie Lodge Alness, Ross-shire IV17 0YH		
4d		From north-east	GLENCALVIE Per Mr Roderick Noble Finlayson Hughes Estate Office, Ardgay, Sutherland	Finlayson Hughes Estate Office Ardgay Sutherland Tel: Ardgay (086 32) 553	
4f	Western Fannichs	Loch a' Bhraoin and north-western approach	BRAEMORE Mr Stokes-Rees 86 Westbourne Park Road London W2 5PL	The Keeper Tel: Lochbroom (085 485) 222	
4e			INVERBROOM Lady Robson Inverbroom Lodge Lochbroom, Ullapool	The Keeper Tel: Lochbroom (085 485) 229	
4m		From south	FANNICH ESTATE Mr W. Baron van Dedem Oude Woudenbergse Zandweg 36 3707 An Zeist, Netherlands	Norrie Matheson Head Stalker Garve Tel: Garve (099 74) 227	Permission obtainable to take car to Fannich Lodge by prior arrangement with estate.

Map/Estate Reference	Mountain or Mountain Group	Approaches	Estate	Contact	Remarks
4m	Eastern Fannichs	Loch Fannich	FANNICH ESTATE Mr W. Baron van Dedem Oude Woudenbergse Zandweg 36 3707 An Zeist, Netherlands	Norrie Matheson Head Stalker Garve Tel: Garve (099 74) 227	Permission obtainable to take car to Fannich Lodge by prior arrangement with estate.
4n		All routes	LOCHLUICHART Lochluichart Estate Co. per Smiths Gore The Square, Fochabers Moray !V32 7DG	K.S. Bowlt Smiths Gore Tel: Fochabers (0343) 820213	
4o	Corriemoillie Forest	Gorstan - Aultguish	CORRIEMIOLLIE Fridays Cranbook Ltd c/o Fountian Forestry Bolgallan, North Kessock	Fountain Forestry North Kessock Tel: Kessock (046 373) 393	
4p	Ben Wyvis	Garbat	WYVIS Mr. B. Coates Wyvis Lodge, Evanton Ross-shire	The Keeper Eileanach Lodge, Evanton Tel: Evanton (0349) 830405	
4i		From north	KILDERMORIE Capt A.D. Hignett Kildermorie Lodge Alness, Ross-shire IV17 0YH		

4q	From west and south	FORESTRY COMMISSION 21 Church Street Inverness IV1 1EL	Easter Ross Forest District Hill Street, Dingwall Ross-shire Tel: Dingwall (0349) 62144

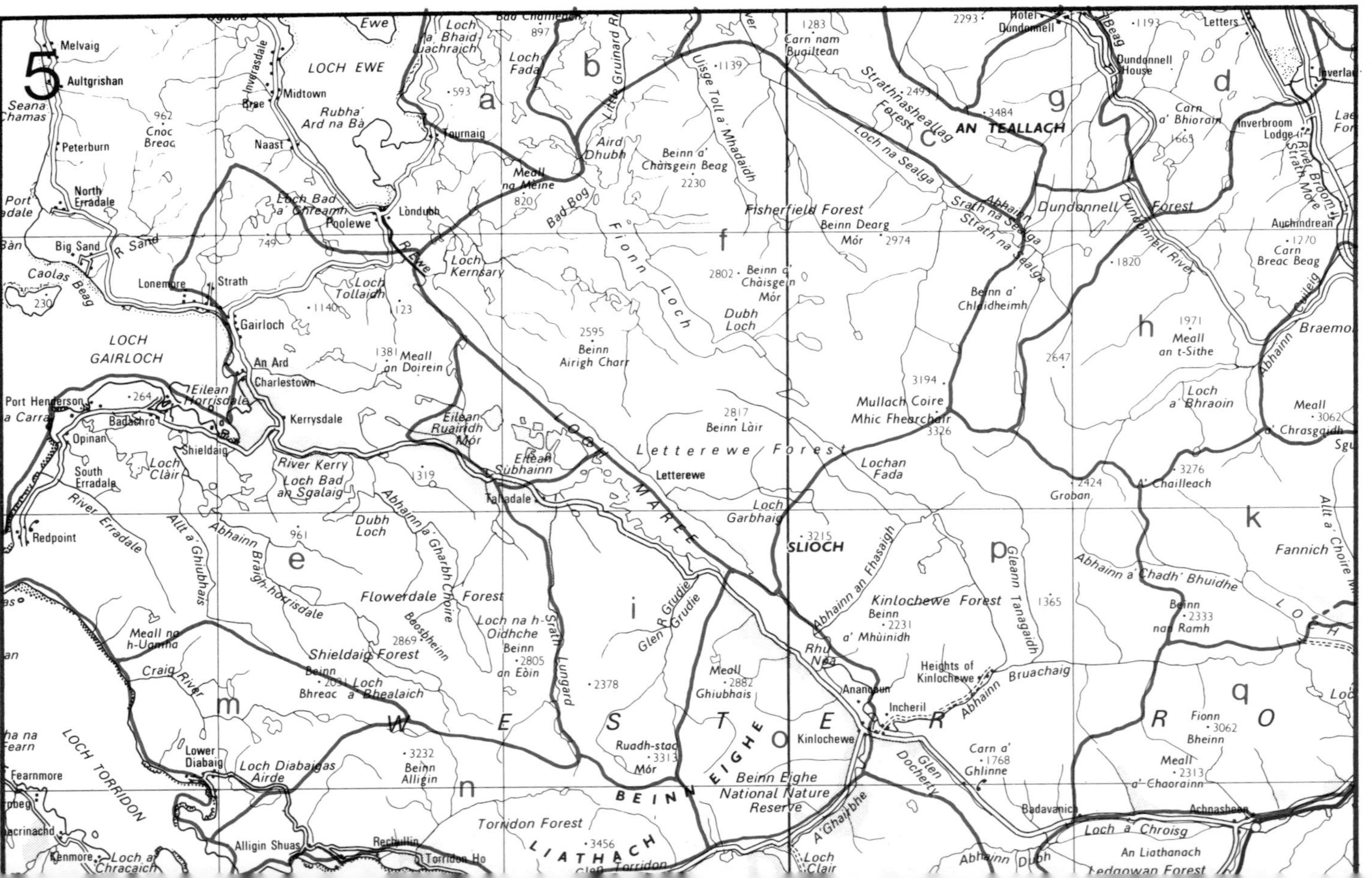

5
LOCH EWE
LOCH GAIRLOCH
LOCH TORRIDON
LOCH MAREE
AN TEALLACH
SLIOCH
BEINN EIGHE
LIATHACH
WESTER ROSS
Fionn Loch
Letterewe Forest
Fisherfield Forest
Strathnasheallag Forest
Dundonnell Forest
Kinlochewe Forest
Flowerdale Forest
Shieldaig Forest
Torridon Forest
Beinn Eighe National Nature Reserve
Poolewe
Gairloch
Kinlochewe
Talladale
Letterewe
Charlestown
Kerrysdale
Badachro
Opinan
Port Henderson
Redpoint
South Erradale
North Erradale
Big Sand
Melvaig
Aultgrishan
Peterburn
Midtown
Naast
Inverasdale
Londubh
Tournaig
Strath
Lonemore
Shieldaig
Lower Diabaig
Alligin Shuas
Fearnmore
Kenmore
Inverbroom Lodge
Dundonnell House
Hotel Dundonnell
Auchindrean
Letters
Incheril
Anancaun
Heights of Kinlochewe
Achnasheen
Badavanich
Glen Docherty
Gleann Tanagaidh
Fannich
Groban
Loch Fada
Loch Kernsary
Loch Tollaidh
Dubh Loch
Lochan Fada
Loch Garbhaig
Loch Clàir
Loch Diabaigas Airde
Loch a' Chroisg
R. Ewe
River Kerry
River Erradale
Craig River
Dundonnell River
River Broom
Strath More
Strath na Sealga
Loch na Sealga
Little Gruinard R.
Uisge Toll a' Mhadaidh
Mullach Coire Mhic Fhearchair
Beinn Dearg Mór
Beinn a' Chàisgein Mór
Beinn a' Chàisgein Beag
Beinn Làir
Beinn Airigh Charr
Meall Ghiubhais
Ruadh-stac Mór
Beinn an Eòin
Beinn Alligin
Baosbheinn
Beinn a' Mhùinidh
Fionn Bheinn
Meall an t-Sithe
Loch a' Bhraoin
An Liathanach
Crown Copyright Reserved

Map 5 — Dundonnell — Torridon

Reference	Estate Name
5a	TOURNAIG
5b	LITTLE GRUINARD
5c	GRUINARD
5d	DUNDONNELL
5e	GAIRLOCH
5f	ARDLAIR/FISHERFIELD/ LETTEREWE
5g	EILEAN DAROCH HOUSE
5h	INVERBROOM
5i	GRUDIE & TALLADALE
5k	FANNICH
5m	DIABAIG
5n	TORRIDON
5o	BEINNE EIGHE NATIONAL NATURE RESERVE
5p	KINLOCHEWE
5q	LOCHROSQUE

Hills

Beinn Airigh Charr
Beinn Lair
Beinn a' Chaisgein Beag
Beinn a' Chaisgein Mor
Beinn Dearg Mor
A' Mhaighdean
Mullach Coire Mhic Fhearchair
An Teallach
Slioch
Beinn a' Mhuinidh
A' Chailleach
Baosbheinn
Beinn an Eoin
Beinn Bhreac
Beinn Alligin
Fionn Bheinn
Beinn Eighe
Liathach

Map/Estate Reference	Mountain or Mountain Group	Approaches	Estate	Contact	Remarks
5f	Beinn Airigh Charr Beinn Lair Beinn a' Chaisgein Beag Beinn a' Chaisgein Mor	All approaches	ARDLAIR/FISHERFIELD/ LETTEREWE Mr Van Vlissingen Ardlair Ross-shire	The Stalker Kernsary Tel: Poolewe (044 586) 215	Locked gate on Kernsary Access. Please keep to existing paths
5a	Beinn Dearg Mor	From north	TOURNAIG Sir John Horlick Bt. Tournaig Poolewe by Achnasheen Ross-shire	Mr Donald J. MacKay Tournaig Farm Tel: Poolewe (044 586) 286	
5b			LITTLE GRUINARD Trustees of the late James D. Lawrie Little Gruinard Estate Laide, by Achnasheen Ross-shire		
5c		From north-east	GRUINARD Countess of Aboyne Gruinard Estate Laide, by Achnasheen Ross-shire IV22 2NQ		

5g		From east	EILEAN DAROCH HOUSE Col. Dumphie Cloquhat, Bridge of Cally Perthshire PH10 7JP	The Keeper Tel: Dundonnell (085 483) 203	
5f	A'Mhaighdean Mullach Coire Mhic Fhearchair	Poolewe approach	ARDLAIR/FISHERFIELD/ LETTEREWE Mr Van Vlissingen Ardlair, Ross-shire	The Stalker Kernsary Tel: Poolewe (044 586) 215	Locked gate on Kernsary access. Please keep to existing paths.
5p		Heights of Kinlochewe approach	KINLOCHEWE Mr H. Whitbread Kinlochewe Estate, Achnasheen	Head Keeper Tel: Kinlochewe (044 584) 247	
5g		From east	EILEAN DAROCH HOUSE Col. Dumphie Cloquhat, Bridge of Cally Perthshire PH10 7JP	The Keeper Tel: Dundonnell (085 483) 203	Gate beside pair of cedar cottages 600yds east of Dundonnell Hotel
5d	An Teallach	From north	DUNDONNELL A.S. Rodger Dundonnell Estate, by Garve Ross-shire	Estate Manager Tel: Dundonnell (085 483) 219	Corrie Hallie to Shenavall path: Eilean Daroch Estate Tel: (085 483) 203
5c		From west	GRUINARD Countess of Aboyne Gruinard Estate Laide, by Achnasheen Ross-shire IV22 2NQ		

Map/Estate Reference	Mountain or Mountain Group	Approaches	Estate	Contact	Remarks
5g		From south	EILEAN DAROCH HOUSE Col. Dumphie Cloquhat, Bridge of Cally Perthshire PH10 7JP	The Keeper Tel: Dundonnell (085 483) 203	
5p	Sloich Beinn a' Mhuinidh	Loch Maree	KINLOCHEWE Mr. H. Whitbread Kinolochewe Estate Achnasheen	Head Keeper Tel: Kinlochewe (044 584) 247	
5f		From north	ARDLAIR/FISHERFIELD/ LETTEREWE Mr Van Vlissingen Ardlair, Ross-shire	The Stalker Kernsary Tel: Poolewe (044 586) 215	Locked gate on Kernsary access. Please keep to existing paths.
5h	A'Chailleach	From north	INVERBROOM Lady Robson Inverbroom Lodge Lochbroom, Ullapool	The Keeper Tel: Lochbroom (085 485) 229	
5p		From south-west	KINLOCHEWE Mr. H. Whitbread Kinlochewe Estate Achnasheen	Head Keeper Tel: Kinlochewe (044 584) 247	

5k		From southeast	FANNICH ESTATE Mr W.Baron van Dedem Oude Woudenbergse Zandweg 36 3707 An Zeist, Netherlands	Norrie Matheson Head Stalker Garve Tel: Garve (099 74) 227	Permission obtainable to take car to Fannich Lodge by prior arrangement with estate.
5e	Baosbheinn Beinn an Eoin Beinn Bhreac Beinn Alligin	Northern approaches	GAIRLOCH J.A. Mackenzie Estates Office Conon Bridge Ross-shire IV7 8AL	Mr A.S. Allan Cathkin An Ard Gairloch, Ross-shire Tel: Gairloch (0445) 2374	
5m		From west	DIABAIG Paul Nicholson 23 Diabaig Torridon, Achnasheen Wester Ross	Ian Mackenzie The Post Office 24 Diabaig Tel: Diabaig (044 581) 220	Part of Gairloch conservation unit for Deer Management.
5n		From south	TORRIDON National Trust for Scotland 5 Charlotte Square Edinburgh EH2 4DL	The Ranger The Mains Torridon Tel: Torridon (044 587) 221	Car parks at entrance to both Coire Dubh and Coire Mhic Nobuil.
5i		From east	GRUDIE & TALLADALE P.J.H. Wills Kirkham Farm Lower Slaughter Cheltenham, Glos.	Nature Conservancy Council Fraser Darling House 9 Culduthel Road Inverness IV2 4AG	

Map/Estate Reference	Mountain or Mountain Group	Approaches	Estate	Contact	Remarks
5q	Fionn Bheinn	Achnasheen	LOCH ROSQUE Mr Pat Wilson Loanleven, Almondbank Perth PH13 NF	The Keeper Tel: Achnasheen (044 588) 266	
5k		From north	FANNICH Mr W. Baron van Dedem Oude Woundenbergse Zandweg 36 3707 An Zeist, Netherlands	Norrie Matheson Head Stalker Tel: Garve (099 74) 227	Permission obtainable to ttake car to Fannich Lodge by arrangment with estate.
5p		From west	KINLOCHEWE Mr H. Whitbread Kinlochewe Achnasheen, Ross-shire	Head Keeper Tel: Kinlochewe (044 584) 247	
5i	Liathach Beinn Eighe	Glen Grudie	GRUDIE & TALLADALE P.J.H. Wills Kirkham Farm Lower Slaughter Cheltenham, Glos.	Nature Conservancy Council Fraser Darling House 9 Culduthel Road Inverness IV2 4AG	

5o	Anancaun Centre Kinlochewe and Loch Bharranch	BEINN EIGHE NATIONAL NATURE RESERVE Nature Conservancy Council Fraser Darling House 9 Culduthel Road Inverness IV2 4AG	Anancaun Visitor Centre Kinlochewe Tel: Kinlochewe (044 584) 254 or 244	
5n	From south and west	TORRIDON National Trust for Scotland 5 Charlotte Square Edinburgh EH2 4DL	The Ranger The Mains Torridon Tel: Torridon (044 587) 221	Car parks at entrance to both Coire Dubh and Coire Mhic Nobuil.

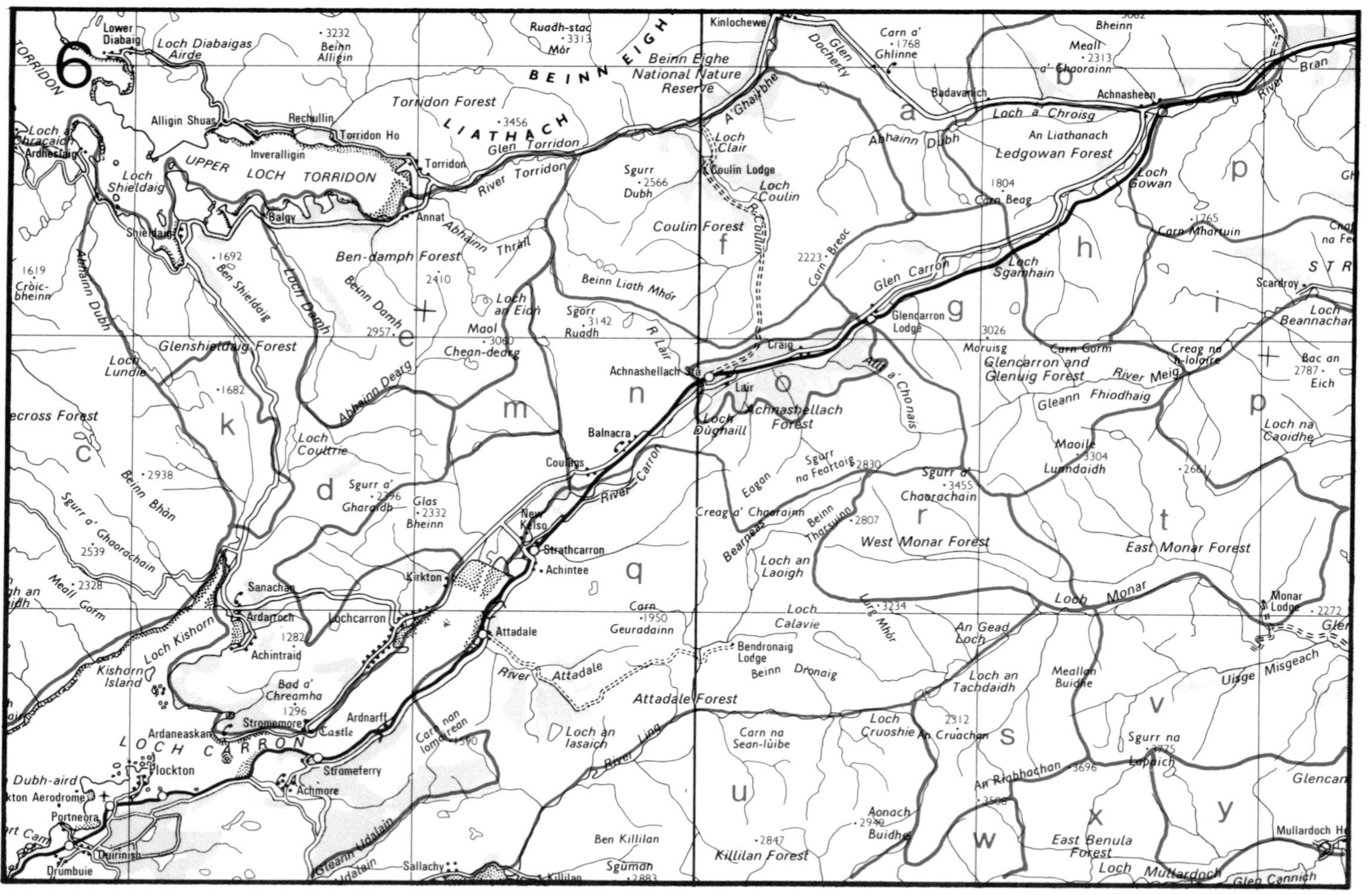
6
TORRIDON
Lower Diabaig
Loch Diabaigas Airde
3232
Beinn Alligin
Ruadh-stac Mór
3313
BEINN EIGHE
Beinn Eighe National Nature Reserve
Kinlochewe
Glen Docherty
Carn a' Ghlinne
1768
Bheinn
Meall a' Chaorainn
2313
Badavanich
Achnasheen
Bran
River
Loch a' Chroisg
An Liathanach
Ledgowan Forest
Abhainn Dubh
A' Ghairbhe
Torridon Forest
LIATHACH
3456
Glen Torridon
Alligin Shuas
Rechullin
Torridon Ho
Inveralligin
Ardheslaig
Loch Shieldaig
UPPER LOCH TORRIDON
Torridon
River Torridon
Balgy
Annat
Shieldaig
Loch Clair
Coulin Lodge
Loch Coulin
R. Coulin
Sgurr Dubh
2566
Coulin Forest
1804
Carn Beag
Loch Gowan
1765
Carn Mhartuin
Abhainn Thrail
Ben-damph Forest
1692
Ben Shieldaig
Loch Damh
Beinn Damh
2410
1619
Cròic-bheinn
Abhainn Dubh
Beinn Liath Mhór
2223
Carn Breac
Glen Carron
Loch Sgamhain
Scardroy
Loch Beannachar
Loch an Eion
Sgorr Ruadh
3142
R. Lair
Glencarron Lodge
3026
Moruisg
Carn Gorm
Creag na h-Iolaire
Bac an Eich
2787
2957
Maol Chean-dearg
3060
Glenshieldaig Forest
Loch Lundie
Craig
Glencarron and Glenuig Forest
River Meig
Achnashellach Sta
Lair
Allt a' Chonais
1682
Abhainn Dearg
Gleann Fhiodhaig
Loch Dùghaill
Achnashellach Forest
Applecross Forest
Loch Coultrie
Balnacra
Loch na Caoidhe
Maoile Lunndaidh
3304
Coulags
Eagan
Sgurr na Feartaig
2830
Sgurr a' Chaorachain
3455
2661
2938
Beinn Bhàn
Sgurr a' Gharaidh
2396
Glas Bheinn
2332
River Carron
Sgurr a' Ghaorachain
2539
New Kelso
Creag a' Chaorainn
Beinn Tharsuinn
2807
West Monar Forest
East Monar Forest
Strathcarron
Bearneas
Achintee
Loch an Laoigh
Kirkton
Meall Gorm
2328
Sanachan
Loch Monar
Monar Lodge
2272
Ardarroch
Lochcarron
Carn Geuradainn
1950
Loch Calavie
3234
Lurg Mhór
An Gead Loch
Loch Kishorn
1282
Attadale
Bendronaig Lodge
Achintraid
River Attadale
Beinn Dronaig
Loch an Tachdaidh
Meallan Buidhe
Uisge Misgeach
Kishorn Island
Bad a' Chreamha
1296
Attadale Forest
Ardnarff
Ardaneaskan
Stromemore
Castle
Carn nan Iomairean
1590
Loch an Iasaich
Carn na Sean-lùibe
Loch Cruoshie
2312
An Cruachan
Sgurr na Lapaich
3775
LOCH CARRON
River Ling
Plockton
Stromeferry
An Riabhachan
3696
Glencannich
Dubh-aird
Plockton Aerodrome
Achmore
3508
Portneora
Aonach Buidhe
2949
Ben Killilan
2847
Killilan Forest
East Benula Forest
Mullardoch Ho
Duirinish
Drumbuie
Gleann Udalain
Sallachy
Killilan
Sgùman
2883
Loch Mullardoch
Glen Cannich

Map 6 — Glen Carron

Reference	Estate Name
6a	KINLOCHEWE
6b	LOCH ROSQUE
6c	APPLECROSS
6d	LOCHCARRON
6e	BEN DAMPH ESTATE
6f	COULIN
6g	GLENCARRON & GLENUIG
6h	LEDGOWAN
6i	SCARDROY
6k	CULDRONAN
6m	NEW KELSO
6n	ACHNASHELLACH
6o	FORESTRY COMMISSION
6p	STRATHCONON
6q	ATTADALE
6r	WEST MONAR
6s	PAIT
6t	MONAR
6u	KILLILAN
6v	BRAULEN
6w	WEST BENULA
6x	EAST BENULA
6y	COZAC

Hills

Beinn Damph
Maol Chean-dearg
Beinn Liath Mhor
Sgorr Ruadh
Applecross Hills
An Riabhachan
Sgurr na Lapaich
Moruisg
Sgurr nan Ceannaichean
Sgurr Choinnich
Sgurr a' Chaorachain
Maoile Lunndaidh
Bidein a' Choire Sheasgaidh
Lurg Mhor

Map/Estate Reference	Mountain or Mountain Group	Approaches	Estate	Contact	Remarks
6e	Beinn Damph Maol Chean-dearg .	Annat and Loch an Eoin	BEN DAMPH ESTATE Messrs T.D. Gray & D.N. Carr-Smith Gt. Yeldham Hall Halstead, Essex	Alistair Holmes 2 Fuaran Torridon Wester Ross Tel: Torridon (044 587) 252	
6m		Coulags	NEW KELSO A.S.Macdonald Torgorm, Conon Bridge, IV7 8DN		
6n			ACHNASHELLACH Major M.T. Wills per Finlayson Hughes 45 Church Street Inverness IV1 1DR	The Stalker Craig Cottage Achnashellach Tel: Achnashellach (052 06) 266	Ample parking on A890 and in the vicinity of Lair.
6d		From south-west	LOCHCARRON Mr. Greg Ash House, Acton Bridge Norwich, Cheshire		
6n	Beinn Liath Mhor Sgorr Ruadh	Achnashellach and Coire Lair	ACHNASHELLACH (as above)	The Stalker (as above)	Ample parking on A890 and in the vicinity of Lair.

6f		Glen Torridon	COULIN Capt. F.H. Wills per Finlayson Hughes 45 Church Street Inverness IV1 1DR	P.J.M. Smith Coulin Estate Kinlochewe Tel: Kinlochewe (044 584) 244	Car park at Coire Dubh. No cars on estate please.
			BEN DAMPH ESTATE Messres T.D. Gray & D.N. Carr-Smith Gt. Yeldham Hall Halstead Essex	Alistair Holmes 2 Fuaran Torridon Wester Ross Tel: Torridon (044 587) 252	
6c	Applecross Hills	All routes	APPLECROSS Capt F.H. Wills per Finlayson Hughes 45 Church Street Inverness IV1 1DR		
6d		From east	LOCHCARRON Mr Greg Ash House, Acton Bridge Norwich, Cheshire		
6k			CULDRONAN Mr Pattenson Culdronan House by Strathcarron Wester Ross		

Map/Estate Reference	Mountain or Mountain Group	Approaches	Estate	Contact	Remarks
6n	Moruisg Sgurr nan Ceannaichean	Craig Allt a' Chonais	ACHNASHELLACH Major M.T. Wills per Finlayson Hughes 45 Church Street Inverness IV1 1DR	The Stalker Craig Cottage Achnashelach Tel: Achnashellach (052 06) 266	Ample parking on A890 and in the vicinity of Lair.
6o			FORESTRY COMMISSION 231 Corstorphine Road Edinburgh	Forest District Manager Strathoich Auchterawe, Fort Augustus Tel: Fort Augustus (0320) 632	
6g		Loch Sgamhain	GLENCARRON AND GLENUIG Glencarron Estate Partnership Glencarron Lodge by Strathcarron Wester Ross	Brian Watson West Cottage Glencarron Lodge by Strathcarron Tel: Achnashellach (052 06) 275	
6h			LEDGOWAN Mr. G. Edward Ruggles-Brise Ledgowan, Achnasheen Ross-shire, IV22 2EH		
6i		From east	SCARDROY		

6n	Sgurr Choinnich Sgurr a' Chaorachain Maoile Lunndaidh	Craig Allt a' Chonais	ACHNASHELLACH Major M.T. Wills per Finlayson Hughes 45 Church Street Inverness IV1 1DR	The Stalker Craig Cottage Achnashellach Tel: Achnashellach (052 06) 266	Ample parking on A890 and in the vicinity of Lair.
6o			FORESTRY COMMISSION 231 Corstorphine Road Edinburgh	Forest District Manager Strathoich, Auchterawe Fort Augustus Tel: Fort Augustus (0320) 6322	
6g		From north	GLENCARRON AND GLENUIG (as above)	Brian Watson (as above)	
6q		From south	ATTADALE E.A. Macpherson Attadale, Strathcarron Wester Ross	T. Watson Stalker's House, Attadale Tel: Lochcarron (052 02) 308	
6r			WEST MONAR C.S.R. Stroyan 15 Atholl Crescent Edinburgh EH3 8HA	Mr D. Lippe Stalker Pait Bheag Monar Tel: Struy (046 376) 267	Only approachable on foot. Please keep to paths along the bottom of the glens.
6t			EAST MONAR David C.R. Allen East Monar, Struy Beauly, Ross-shire		

Map/Estate Reference	Mountain or Mountain Group	Approaches	Estate	Contact	Remarks
6p		From east	STRATHCONON A.J. Macdonald-Buchanan Srathconon House Muir of Ord Ross-shire	C. Hendry Head Stalker Achlorachan House Tel: Strathconon (099 77) 207	Vehicles should not be parked so as to block hill tracks. Take notice of warning signs erected at access to hill land.
6q	Bidein a' Choire Sheasgiadh Lurg Mhor	Achintee and Attadale to Bearnais	ATTADALE (as above)	T. Watson (as above)	
6r		From north-east	WEST MONAR (as above)	Mr D. Lippe (as above)	Only appoachable on foot Please keep to paths along the bottom of the glens.
6u		From south	KILLILAN Smech Properties per Mr R. Carr Inverinate Estate Office Kyle, Wester Ross	The Keeper Killilan Tel: Killilan (059 988) 262	
6s	An Riabhachan Sgurr na Lapaich	From north and west	PAIT C.S.R. Stroyan 15 Atholl Cresent Edinburgh, EH3 8HA	Mr D. Lippe Stalker Pait Bheag Tel: Struy (046 376) 267	Only apporachable on foot Please keep to paths along the bottom of the glens.

6v	From north and east	BRAULEN Lovat Estates per Simon Foster Estate Office Beauly, Ross-shire	The Gatekeeper Tel: Struy (046 376) 260 or NCC Warden (046 376) 310	An agreement between the NCC and landowner allows walkers to obtain gate key from NCC rep. who lives by gate.
6w	From south	WEST BENULA Smech Properties per Mr R. Carr Inverinate Estate Office Kyle, Wester Ross		
6x		EAST BENULA Carl Lawaetz East Benula Glen Cannich Beauly IV4 7LX		
6y	From south-east	COZAC Carl Lawaetz East Benula Glen Cannich Beauly IV4 7LX		

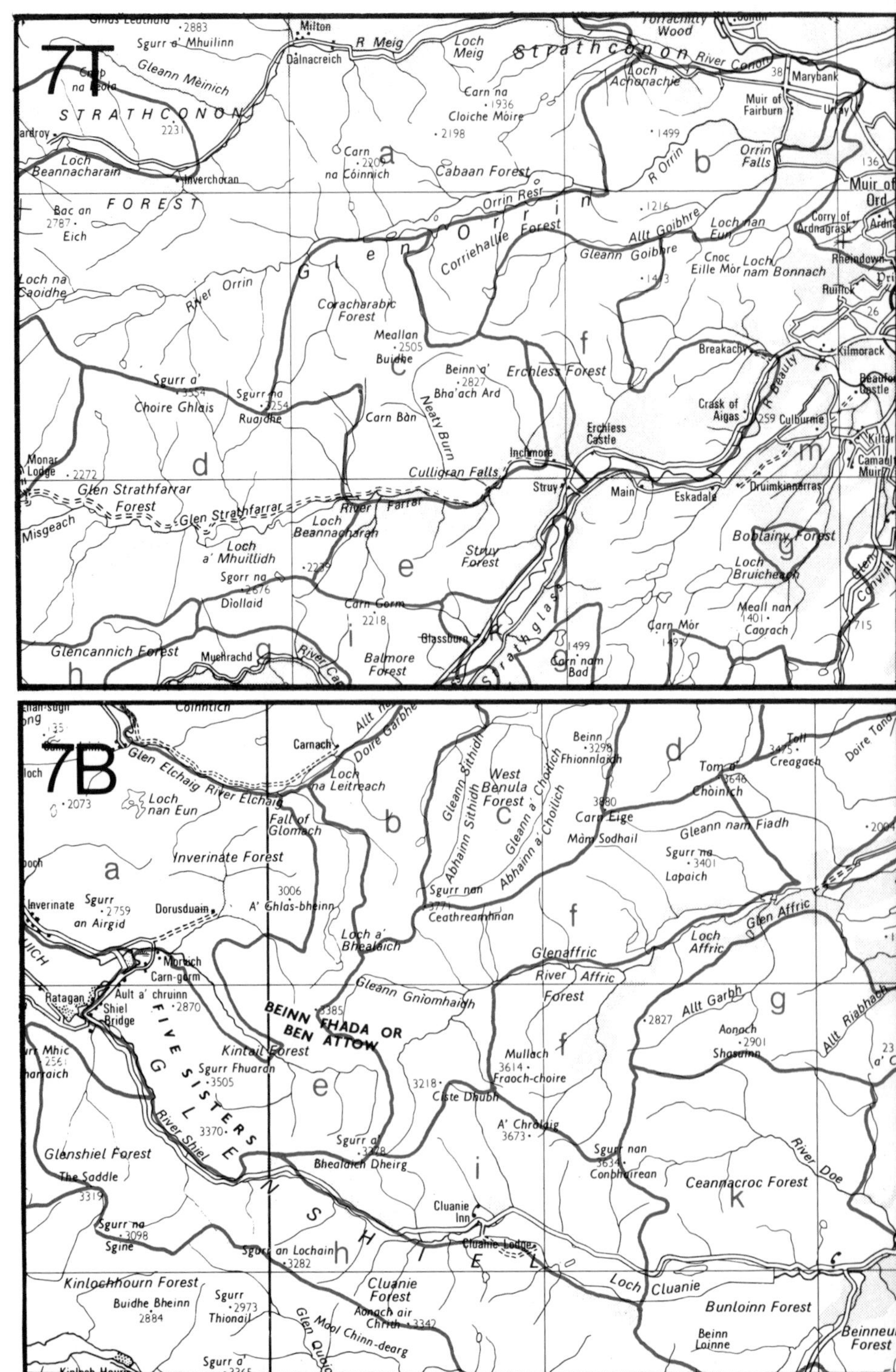

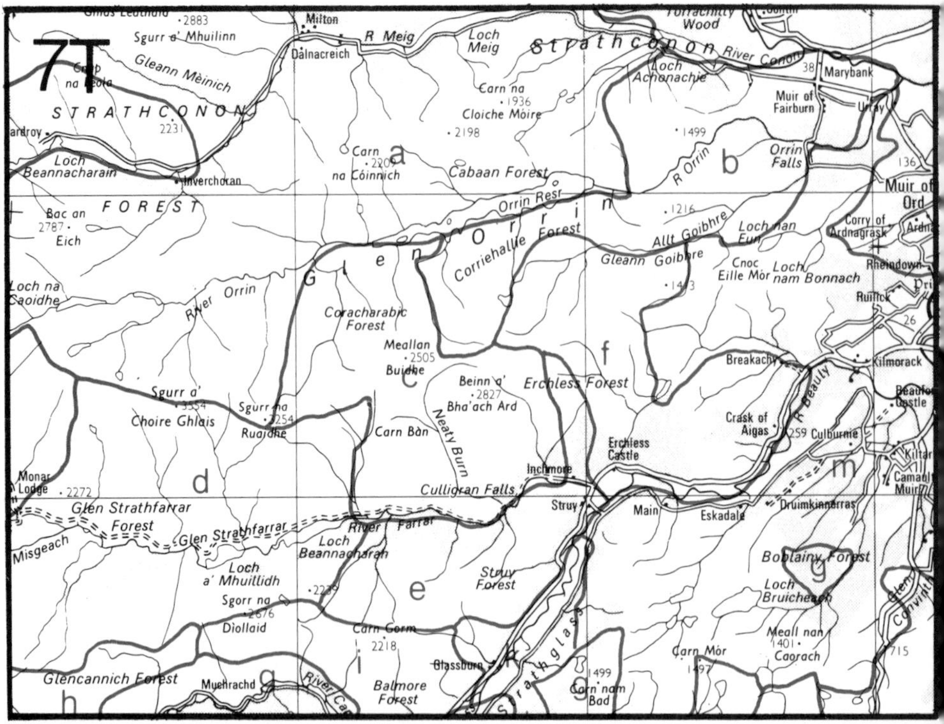
7T
Sgurr a' Mhuilinn
Milton
R Meig
Dalnacreich
Loch Meig
Strathconon
River Conon
Loch Achonachie
Marybank
Muir of Fairburn
Urray
Glenn Mèinich
STRATHCONON
FOREST
Loch Beannacharain
Inverchoran
Carn na Cloiche Mòire
Carn na Cóinnich
Cabaan Forest
Orrin Rest
R Orrin
Orrin Falls
Muir of Ord
Bac an Eich
Glen Orrin
Corriehallie Forest
Allt Goibhre
Gleann Goibhre
Loch nan Eun
Corry of Ardnagrask
Cnoc Eille Mòr
Loch nam Bonnach
Rheindown
Ruilick
Loch na Caoidhe
River Orrin
Coracharabic Forest
Meallan Buidhe
Beinn a' Bha'ach Ard
Erchless Forest
Breakachy
Kilmorack
Beaufort Castle
Sgurr a' Choire Ghlais
Sgurr na Ruaidhe
Carn Bàn
Neaty Burn
Crask of Aigas
R Beauly
Culburnie
Erchless Castle
Inchmore
Monar Lodge
Culligran Falls
Struy
Main
Eskadale
Druimkinnerras
Glen Strathfarrar Forest
Glen Strathfarrar
River Farrar
Misgeach
Loch Beannacharan
Loch a' Mhuillidh
Boblainy Forest
Loch Bruicheach
Sgorr na Diollaid
Struy Forest
Carn Gorm
Meall nan Caorach
Carn Mór
Glassburn
Strathglass
Glencannich Forest
Muchrachd
Balmore Forest
Corn nam Bad

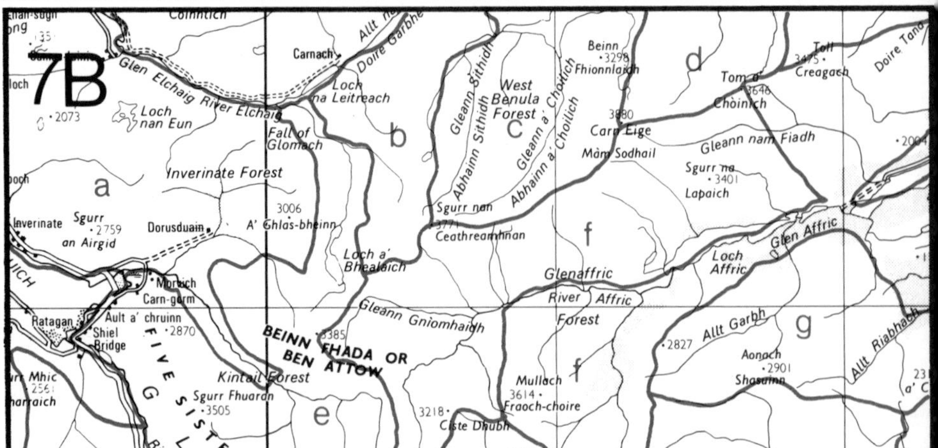
7B
Carnach
Allt na Doire Garbhe
Glen Elchaig
River Elchaig
Loch na Leitreach
Loch nan Eun
Fall of Glomach
Gleann Sithidh
Abhainn Sithidh
West Benula Forest
Gleann a' Choilich
Abhainn a' Choilich
Beinn Fhionnlaidh
Carn Eige
Màm Sodhail
Tom a' Chòinich
Toll Creagach
Gleann nam Fiadh
Sgurr na Lapaich
Inverinate Forest
Inverinate
Sgurr an Airgid
Dorusduain
A' Ghlas-bheinn
Sgurr nan Ceathreamhnan
Glen Affric
Loch Affric
Loch a' Bhealaich
Glenaffric
River Affric
Forest
Morvich
Carn-gorm
Ault a' chruinn
Ratagan
Shiel Bridge
Gleann Gniomhaidh
BEINN FHADA OR BEN ATTOW
Allt Garbh
Allt Riabhach
Aonach Shasuinn
FIVE SISTERS
Kintail Forest
Sgurr Fhuaran
Mullach Fraoch-choire
Ciste Dhubh
A' Chràlaig
River Shiel
Glenshiel Forest
The Saddle
Sgurr a' Bhealaich Dheirg
Sgurr nan Conbhairean
Ceannacroc Forest
River Doe
GLEN SHIEL
Cluanie Inn
Cluanie Lodge
Sgurr na Sgine
Sgurr an Lochain
Loch Cluanie
Kinlochhourn Forest
Buidhe Bheinn
Sgurr Thionail
Cluanie Forest
Aonach air Chrith
Maol Chinn-dearg
Glen Quoich
Bunloinn Forest
Beinn Loinne
Beinneun Forest

Map 7T — Stathconon — Strathfarrar

Reference	Estate Name
7T/a	STRATHCONON
7T/b	FAIRBURN & CORRIEHALLIE
7T/c	CULLIGRAN
7T/d	BRAULEN
7T/e	STRUY
7T/f	ERCHLESS
7T/g	FORESTRY COMMISSION
7T/h	COZAC
7T/i	BALMORE
7T/k	GLASS BURN
7T/m	LOVAT ESTATES

Hills

Strathconon Hills
Glen Orrin
Sgurr a' Choire Ghlais Group
Meallan Buidhe
Beinn a' Bha'ach Ard
Carn Ban
Sgurr na Diollaid
Carn Gorm

Map 7B — Kintail — Affric

Reference	Estate Name
7B/a	INVERINATE
7B/b	GLOMACH
7B/c	WEST BENULA
7B/d	EAST BENULA
7B/e	KINTAIL
7B/f	FORESTRY COMMISSION
7B/g	OLD GUISACHAN
7B/h	GLENSHIEL & CLUANIE
7B/i	CORRIELAIR
7B/k	CEANNACROC

Hills

Sgurr an Airgid
Sgurr nan Ceathreamhnan
Carn Eige
Mam Sodhail
Sgurr na Lapaich
Beinn Fhada or Ben Attow
Five Sisters of Kintail
Saileag
Sgurr a' Bhealaich Dheirg
Ciste Dhubh Group
A' Chralaig
Sgurr nan Conbhairean

Map/Estate Reference	Mountain or Mountain Group	Approaches	Estate	Contact	Remarks
7T/a	Strathconon Hills Glen Orrin	From Strathanmore and Inverchoran	STRATHCONON A.J. Macdonald-Buchanan Strathconon House Strathconon, Muir of Ord Ross-shire	C. Hendry Head Stalker Achlorachan House Strathconon Tel: Strathconon (099 77) 207	Vehicles should not be parked so as to block hill tracks. Take notice of warning signs erected at access to hill land.
7T/b		From north-east	FAIRBURN AND CORRIEHALLIE R.W.K. Stirling, Arcan Muir of Ord, IV6 7UL	R.W.K. Stirling Tel: Urray (099 73) 273/4 or Norman Kelman Tel: Urray (099 73) 243	Please park at Aultgowrie or gate on road to Achederson Farm.
7T/c		From south	CULLIGRAN C. Frank Spencer Nairn Culligran House, Struy IV4 7JX	C. Frank Spencer Nairn Tel: Muir of Ord (0463) 76285	Parking at Leishmore
7T/a	Sgurr a' Choire Ghlais Group	From north	STRATHCONON (as above)	C. Hendry (as above)	
7T/d		From Glen Strathfarrar	BRAULEN per Simon Foster Lovat Estates Estate Office Beauly, Ross-shire	The Gatekeeper Tel: Struy (046 376) 260 or NCC Warden (046 374) 310	An agreement between tha landowner and NCC allows walkers to obatin gate key form NCC rep. who lives by the gate.

7T/c		From east	CULLIGRAN (as above)	C. Frank Spencer (as above)	
7T/c	Meallan Buidhe Beinn a' Bha'ach Ard Carn Ban	All routes	CULLIGRAN C. Frank Spencer Nairn Culligran House Struy, IV4 7JX	C.Frank Spencer Nairn Tel: Muir of Ord (0463) 76285	Parking at Leishmore.
7T/b		From north	FAIRBURN AND CORRIEHALLIE R.W.K. Stirling Arcan Muir of Ord IV6 7UL	R.W.K. Stirling Tel: Urray (099 73) 273/4 or Norman Kelman Tel: Urray (099 73) 243	Please park at Aultgowrie or gate on road to Achederson Farm.
7T/f		From north-east	ERCHLESS		
7T/d		From south-west	BRAULEN per Simon Foster Lovat Estates Estate Office Beauly, Ross-shire	The Gatekeeper Tel: Struy (046 376) 260 or NCC Warden (046 374) 310	An agreement between the landowner and NCC allows walkers to obtain gate key from NCC rep who lives by the gate.
7T/d	Sgurr na Diollaid Carn Gorm	From north	BRAULEN (as above)	The Gatekeeper (as above)	
7T/g		From south	FORESTRY COMMISSION 231 Corstorphine Road Edinburgh EH12 7AT	Forest District Manager Strathoich Fort Augustus Tel: Fort Augustus (0320) 6322	

Map/Estate Reference	Mountain or Mountain Group	Approaches	Estate	Contact	Remarks
7T/h		From west	COZAC Carl Lawaetz East Benula, Glen Cannich Beauly IV4 7LX	Tel: Cannich (045 65) 347	
7T/e		From north and east	STRUY Over Rankeilour Farms Ltd Angus Spencer Nairn Struy, Beauly Ross-shire	Henry Bain Stalker Struy Tel: Struy (046 376) 276	
7T/i			BALMORE Carl Lawaetz East Benula, Glen Cannich Beauly IV4 7LX	Tel: Cannich (045 65) 339	
7B/a	Sgurr an Airgid	All approaches	INVERINATE Smech Properties per Mr. R. Carr Inverinate Estate Office Kyle, Wester Ross		
7B/e	Sgurr nan Ceathreamhnan	From west (Glen Lichd)	KINTAIL National Trust for Scotland 5 Charlotte Square Edinburgh EH2 4DU	NTS Ranger Morvich Tel: Glenshiel (059 981) 219	

7B/a		Glen Elchaig	INVERINATE (as above)	
7B/b			GLOMACH Smech Properties per Mr. R. Carr Inverinate Estate Office Kyle, Wester Ross	
7B/f		Glen Affric	FORESTRY COMMISSION 21 Church Street Inverness IV1 1EL	Forest District Manager Strathoich Fort Augustus Tel: Fort Augustus (0320) 6322
7B/c		From north	WEST BENULA Smech Properties per Mr R. Carr Inverinate Estate Office Kyle, Wester Ross	
7B/d			EAST BENULA Carl Lawaetz East Benula, Glen Cannich Beauly IV4 7LX	
7B/f	Carn Eige Mam Sodhail	Glen Affric	FORESTRY COMMISSION 21 Church Street Inverness IV1 1EL	Forest District Manager Strathoich Fort Augustus Tel: Fort Augustus (0320) 6322

Map/Estate Reference	Mountain or Mountain Group	Approaches	Estate	Contact	Remarks
7B/d		Gleann a' Choilich	EAST BENULA Carl Lawaetz (as above)		
7B/c			WEST BENULA Smech Properties per Mr R. Carr Inverinate Estate Office Kyle, Wester Ross		
7B/e	Beinn Fhada or Ben Attow Five Sisters Saileag Sgurr a' Bhealaich Dheirg Ciste Dhubh Group	Glen Shiel, Glen Lichd	KINTAIL National Trust for Scotland 5 Charlotte Square Edinburgh EH2 4DU	NTS Ranger Morvich Tel: Glenshiel (059 981) 219	
7B/f		From north-east	FORESTRY COMMISSION (as above)	Forest District Manager (as above)	
7B/i		From south-east	CORRIELAIR	Tel: Dalchreichart (0320) 40237 and (0320) 40246	

7B/i	A' Chralaig Sgurr nan Conbhairean	From Loch Cluanie	CORRIELAIR (as above)	(as above)
7B/k			CEANNACROC Messrs T.D. Girvan & Sons Ceannacroc Estate Glenmoriston IV3 6YN	Tel: Dalchreichart (0320) 40243
7B/f		From north	FORESTRY COMMISSION 21 Church Street Inverness IV1 1EL	Forest District Manager Strathoich Fort Augustus Tel: Fort Augustus (0320) 6322
7B/g			OLD GUISACHAN	

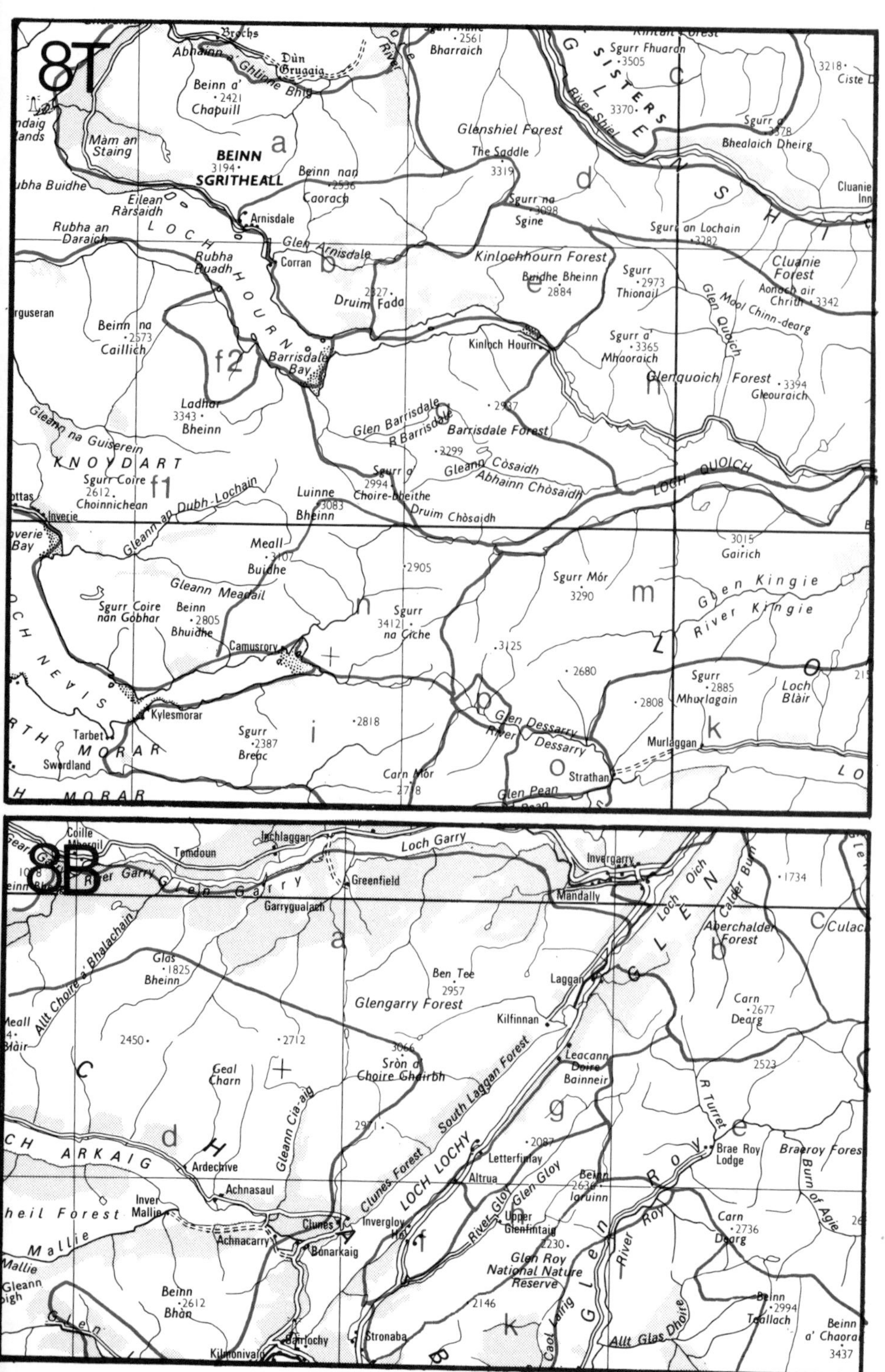
8T
Brochs
Abhainn a' Ghlinne Bhig
Dùn Gruggaig
Beinn a' Chapuill
2421
2561
Bharraich
Sgurr Fhuaran
3505
SISTERS
GLEN SHIEL
River Shiel
3370
3218
Ciste D
Sgurr a'
3378
Bhealaich Dheirg
Màm an Staing
BEINN SGRITHEALL
3194
Glenshiel Forest
The Saddle
3319
Rubha Buidhe
Beinn nan Caorach
2536
Eilean Ràrsaidh
Arnisdale
Sgurr na Sgine
3098
Cluanie Inn
Rubha an Daraich
LOCH HOURN
Glen Arnisdale
Sgurr an Lochain
3282
Rubha Ruadh
Corran
Kinlochhourn Forest
Buidhe Bheinn
2884
Sgurr Thionail
2973
Cluanie Forest
Druim Fada
2327
Aonach air Chrith
3342
Glen Quoich
Mool Chinn-dearg
Beinn na Caillich
2573
Kinloch Hourn
Sgurr a' Mhaoraich
3365
Barrisdale Bay
Glenquoich Forest
3394
Gleouraich
Ladhar Bheinn
3343
2937
Glen Barrisdale
R Barrisdale
Barrisdale Forest
Gleann na Guiserein
KNOYDART
3299
Gleann Còsaidh
Abhainn Chòsaidh
Sgurr Coire Choinnichean
2612
Sgurr a' Choire-bheithe
2994
LOCH QUOICH
Luinne Bheinn
3083
Druim Chòsaidh
Inverie
Gleann an Dubh-Lochain
Inverie Bay
Meall Buidhe
3107
3015
Gairich
2905
Sgurr Mór
3290
Glen Kingie
River Kingie
Gleann Meadail
Sgurr Coire nan Gobhar
Beinn Bhuidhe
2805
Sgurr na Ciche
3412
3125
Camusrory
LOCH NEVIS
2680
Sgurr Mhurlagain
2885
Loch Blàir
Kylesmorar
2808
Glen Dessarry
River Dessarry
Tarbet
Sgurr Breac
2387
2818
Murlaggan
MORAR
Swordland
Strathan
Carn Mór
2718
Glen Pean
8B
Coille Mhorgil
Inchlaggan
Loch Garry
Tomdoun
Invergarry
River Garry
Glen Garry
Greenfield
1734
Mandally
Garrygualach
Loch Oich
Calder Burn
GLEN
Aberchalder Forest
Culach
Allt Choire a' Bhalachain
Glas Bheinn
1825
Ben Tee
2957
Laggan
Glengarry Forest
Carn Dearg
2677
Kilfinnan
2450
2712
3066
Leacann Doire Bainneir
Sròn a' Choire Ghairbh
Geal Charn
2523
South Laggan Forest
R Turret
Gleann Cia-aig
2971
2087
LOCH ARKAIG
LOCH LOCHY
Letterfinlay
Brae Roy Lodge
Braeroy Forest
Ardechive
Clunes Forest
Altrua
Glen Gloy
Beinn Iaruinn
2636
Achnasaul
Inver Mallie
Burn of Agie
Clunes
Invergloy
River Gloy
Upper Glenfintaig
Carn Dearg
2736
Mallie
Achnacarry
Bunarkaig
2230
River Roy
Glen Roy National Nature Reserve
Glen Roy
Beinn Bhàn
2612
2146
Beinn Teallach
2994
Caol Lairig
Allt Glas Dhoire
Beinn a' Chaorainn
3437
Bunarkaig
Stronaba
Kilmonivaig

Map 8T — Knoydart

Reference	Estate Name
8T/a	EILEANREACH
8T/b	ARNISDALE
8T/c	KINTAIL
8T/d	GLENSHIEL & CLUANIE
8T/e	KINLOCH HOURN
8T/f	KNOYDART (1)
8T/f	KNOYDART (2) LI & COIRE DHORRCAIL
8T/g	BARRISDALE
8T/h	WESTER GLENQUOICH
8T/i	NORTH MORAR
8T/k	LOCHEIL ESTATES
8T/m	FORESTRY COMMISSION
8T/n	CAMUSRORY
8T/o	GLENPEAN
8T/p	GLENDESSARY

Hills

Beinn Sgritheall
South Glen Shiel Ridge
The Saddle
Sgurr a' Mhaoraich
Gleouraich
Spidean Mialach
Buidhe Bheinn
Sgurr Thionail
Beinn na Caillich
Ladhar Bheinn
Sgurr Coire Choinnichean
Luinne Bheinn
Meall Buidhe
Sgurr na Ciche
Sgurr Mor
Gairich
Glen Kingie

Map 8B — Loch Arkaig to Glen Garry

Reference	Estate Name
8B/a	FORESTRY COMMISSION
8B/b	ABERCHALDER
8B/c	CULACHY
8B/d	LOCHEIL ESTATES
8B/e	BRAEROY
8B/f	INVERGLOY
8B/g	LETTERFINLAY
8B/h	GLENFINTAIG
8B/i	GLEN ROY NATIONAL NATURE RESERVE
8B/k	FORESTRY COMMISSION

Hills

Glas Bheinn
Meall na Teanga
Sron a' Choire Ghairbh
Ben Tee
Carn Dearg
Upper Glen Roy Hills
Glen Gloy
Glen Roy

Map/Estate Reference	Mountain or Mountain Group	Approaches	Estate	Contact	Remarks
8T/a	Beinn Sgritheall	All routes	EILEANREACH Hon. G.M.H. Wills Oversley Castle Farm Wixford, Alcester Warwickshire	Tel: Glenelg (059 982) 312 and (059 982) 244	
8T/b		Arnisdale	ARNISDALE Wakefield Lodge Potterspury, Northants	J.H. Richmond-Watson Tel: Paulerspury (032 733) 218 or Tel: Glenelg (059 982) 216	Parking at Corran.
8T/d	South Glen Shiel Ridge and The Saddle Sgurr a' Mhaoraich Gleouraich and Spidean Mialach Buidhe Bheinn	Glen Shiel	GLENSHIEL & CLUANIE Burton Property Trustees Dochfour Estates Office Inverness	Ian Campbell Estate Manager Shiel House Tel: Glenshiel (059 981) 282	
8T/b	Sgurr Thionail	From south	ARNISDALE (as above)	J.H.Richmond-Watson (as above)	
8T/e			KINLOCH HOURN Henry C. Birbeck Estate Office Westacre Kings Lynn, Norfolk	Donald Cameron Stalkers Cottage Kinloch Hourn Invergarry Tel: Tomdoun (080 92) 236	Car park at Loch Hourn Head.

8T/h			WESTER GLENQUOICH Major Gordon, Lude Farm Blair Atholl Perthshire	Tel: Blair Atholl (079 681) 240
8T/f	Beinn na Caillich Ladhar Bheinn Sgurr Coire Choinnichean Luinne Bheinn Meall Buidhe	All routes	KNOYDART (1) Mr Phillip Rhodes Regal House Station Approach Haslemere, Surrey.	Head Keeper Donald MaCleugash Tel: Mallaig (0687) 2000
			KNOYDART (2) LI AND COIRE DHORRCAIL John Muir Trust per The Secretary 5 Gray Street, Broughty Ferry Dundee DD5 2BH	
8T/g		From east	BARRISDALE Major Gordon Lude Farm, Blair Atholl Perthshire	Tel: Blair Atholl (079 681) 240
8T/n	Sgurr na Ciche Sgurr Mor Gairich Glen Kingie	All routes	CAMUSRORY	

Map/Estate Reference	Mountain or Mountain Group	Approaches	Estate	Contact	Remarks
8T/f		From north and west	KNOYDART (1) Mr Phillip Rhodes Regal House Station Approach Haslemere, Surrey	Head Keeper Donald MacCleugash Tel: Mallaig (0687) 2000	
8T/f			KNOYDART (2) LI AND COIRE DHORRCAIL (as above)		
8T/g			BARRISDALE Major Gordon Lude Farm Blair Atholl, Perthshire	Tel: Blair Atholl ((079 681) 240	
8T/i		From south	NORTH MORAR Mrs. I.R.S. Bond North Morar Estate Swordlands Mallaig PH40 4PE		
8T/o			GLENPEAN Post Office Pension Fund c/o Fountain Forestry Bogallan Nursery North Kessock, Inverness	Ian Gillies Tulloch Roybridge Tel: Tulloch (039 785) 251	

8T/p			GLENDESSARY Mrs C. Kroch Rhodes c/o Fountain Forestry Bogallan Nursery North Kessock, Inverness	Ian Gillies Tulloch Roybridge Tel: Tulloch (039 785) 251
8T/k		Quoich, Kingie	LOCHEIL ESTATES Donald Angus Cameron Ygr. of Locheil, Achnacarry Spean Bridge	West Highland Estates Office 33 High Street Fort William Tel: Fort William (0397) 2433
8T/m			FORESTRY COMMISSION 21 Church Street Inverness IV1 1EL	Lochaber Forest District Torlundy, Fort William Tel: Fort William (0397) 2184
8B/d	Glas Bheinn Meall na Teanga Sron a' Choire Ghairbh Ben Tee	Loch Lochy Carn Bhealach	LOCHEIL ESTATES Donald Angus Cameron Ygr. of Locheil Achnancarry Spean Bridge	West Highland Estates Office 33 High Street Fort William Tel: Fort William (0397) 2433
8B/a			FORESTRY COMMISSION 21 Church Street Inverness IV1 1EL	Lochaber Forest District Torlundy, Fort William Tel: Fort William (0397) 2184

Map/Estate Reference	Mountain or Mountain Group	Approaches	Estate	Contact	Remarks
8B/b	Carn Dearg and Upper Glen Roy Hills	From north	ABERCHALDER Miss Jean Ellice Taigh-an-Lianach Aberchalder Farm Invergarry PH35 4HN	Miss Jean Ellice Tel: Invergarry (080 93) 287 or Mr Wernham Tel: Invergarry (080 93) 373	Parking by prior arrangement only.
8B/e		Carn Bhrunachan	BRAEROY Mr Buckle per Finlayson Hughes The Square Aberfeldy, Perthshire	Gordon Addison Keepers Cottage Braeroy, Roybridge Tel: Spean Bridge (039 781) 210	Parking in lay-by close to footbridge in Glen Roy.
8B/g		Glen Gloy	LETTERFINLAY	Ronnie Mackintosh Shepherd	
8B/i		From south and Glen Roy	GLEN ROY NATIONAL NATURE RESERVE Nature Conservancy Council NW Region Fraser Darling House Culduthel Road, Inverness		
8B/h	Glen Gloy Glen Roy	From south	GLENFINTAIG		

8B/f	INVERGLOY	
8B/g	LETTERFINLAY	
8B/k	FORESTRY COMMISSION 21 Church Street Inverness IV1 1EL	Lochaber Forest District Torlundy, Fort William Tel: Fort William (0397) 2184
8B/i	GLEN ROY NATIONAL NATURE RESERVE (as above)	

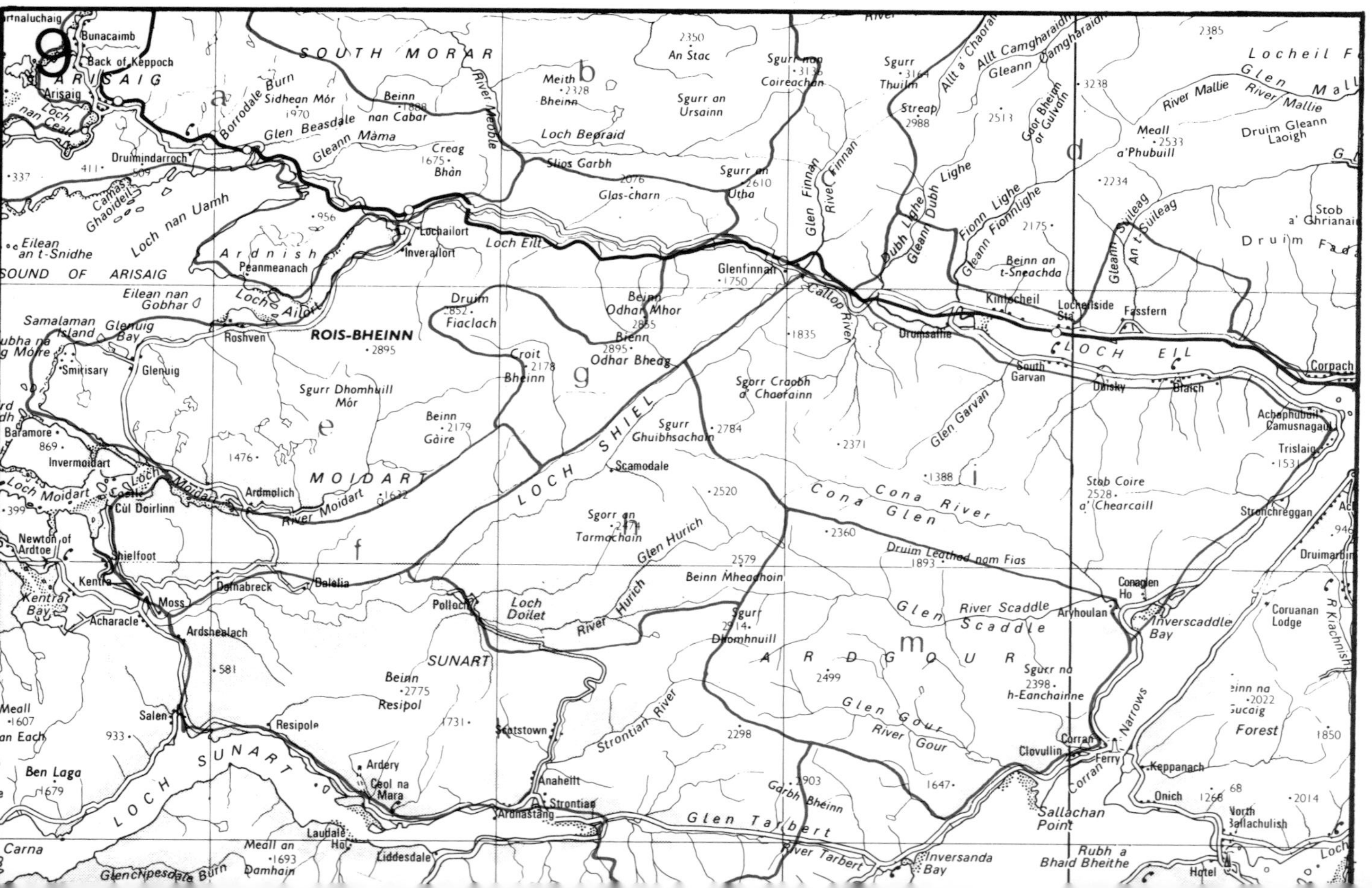

SOUTH MORAR
River Meoble
ARISAIG
Arisaig
Back of Keppoch
Bunacaimb
Loch nan Ceall
Loch nan Uamh
SOUND OF ARISAIG
Eilean nan Gobhar
Ardnish
Peanmeanach
Loch Ailort
Lochailort
Inverailort
Loch Eilt
Glen Beasdale
Gleann Màma
Borrodale Burn
Drumindarroch
ROIS-BHEINN
Roshven
Glenuig
Samalaman Island
Smirisary
Sgurr Dhomhuill Mór
Loch Moidart
Invermoidart
Cùl Doirlinn
MOIDART
River Moidart
Ardmolich
Dalnabreck
Dalelia
Acharacle
Shielfoot
Kentra Bay
Newton of Ardtoe
Salen
Ardshealach
LOCH SUNART
SUNART
Resipole
Beinn Resipol
Ardery
Ceol na Mara
Liddesdale
Laudale Ho
Strontian
Anaheilt
Scotstown
Ardnastang
Strontian River
Polloch
Loch Doilet
River Hurich
Glen Hurich
LOCH SHIEL
Scamodale
Glenfinnan
Callop River
Glen Finnan
River Finnan
Meith Bheinn
Loch Beoraid
Slios Garbh
Glas-charn
An Stac
Sgurr an Ursainn
Sgurr Thuilm
Streap
Gleann Dubh Lighe
Gleann Fionnlighe
Beinn an t-Sneachda
Druimsallie
Kinlocheil
LOCH EIL
Locheilside Sta
Fassfern
Corpach
Duisky
Blaich
South Garvan
Glen Garvan
Cona Glen
Cona River
Druim Leathad nam Fias
Beinn Mheadhoin
ARDGOUR
Glen Scaddle
River Scaddle
Glen Gour
River Gour
Glen Tarbert
River Tarbert
Garbh Bheinn
Inversanda Bay
Inverscaddle Bay
Conaglen Ho
Aryhoulan
Clovullin
Corran
Ferry
Sallachan Point
Corran Narrows
Onich
Keppanach
North Ballachulish
Coruanan Lodge
R Kiachnish
Stronchreggan
Trislaig
Achaphubuil
Camusnagaul
Glen Mallie
River Mallie
Druim Gleann Laoigh
Meall a'Phubuill
Locheil Forest
Ben Laga
Carna

Map 9 — Glenfinnan — Ardgour

Reference	Estate Name
9a	ARISAIG
9b	MEOBLE & LETTERMORAR
9c	GLENFINNAN
9d	LOCHEIL
9e	INVERAILORT
9f	LOCH SHIEL
9g	GLENALADALE
9h	FORESTRY COMMISSION
9i	CONA GLEN
9k	SUNART
9m	ARDGOUR

Hills

Arisaig
South Morar
Glenfinnan
Streap
Gulvain
Sgurr nan Coireachan
Sgurr Thuilm
Ardgour
Rois-Bheinn
Moidart
Beinn Resipol

Map/Estate Reference	Mountain or Mountain Group	Approaches	Estate	Contact	Remarks
9a	Arisaig - South Morar	All routes	ARISAIG E. & E. MacMillan per West Highland Estates Office 33 High Street, Fort William	E.D.MacMillan Borrodale Farm Arisaig Tel: Arisaig (068 75) 229	
9c	Glenfinnan Hills Streap Gulvain	From south	GLENFINNAN Mr Wallis per Economic Forestry Ltd 20 High Street, Fort William	The Stalker Tel: Kinlocheil (039 783) 270	
9d		From east	LOCHEIL ESTATES Donald Angus Cameron Ygr. of Locheil Achnacarry Spean Bridge	West Highland Estate Office 33 High Street Fort William Tel: Fort William (0397) 2433	
9b	Sgurr nan Coireachan Sgurr Thuilm	From west and south-west	MEOBLE & LETTERMORAR Miss Ford Meoble Lodge Morar		
9c		From south	GLENFINNAN (as above)	The Stalker (as above)	

9/e	Rois-Bheinn Moidart	All routes	INVERAILORT Mrs Cameron Head Inverailort Castle Inverailort		
9/f		From south	LOCHSHIEL The Westminster (Liverpool) Trust per West Highland Estates Office 33 High Street, Fort William	D. Shankland Keeper's Cottage Dorlin, Acharacle Argyll Tel: Salen (096 785) 618	
9/g		From west	GLENALADALE		
9/i	Ardgour Group	Cona Glen	CONA GLEN J. Guthrie Esq per West Highland Estates Office 33 High Street, Fort William	R.T. Sidgwick West Highland Estates Office Tel: Fort William (0397) 2433	
9/m		Glen Scaddle Glen an-lochain Dubh	ARDGOUR Miss Maclean of Ardgour Ardgour House Ardgour by Fort William	R.M. Maclean of Ardgour Sallachan Farm, Ardgour Tel: Ardgour (085 55) 247	Footpath through Glengour to Strontian. Please keep to paths.
9/h		From west	FORESTRY COMMISSION 21 Church Street Inverness IV1 1EL	Lochaber Forest District Torlundy, Fort William Tel: Fort William (0397) 2184	

Map/Estate Reference	Mountain or Mountain Group	Approaches	Estate	Contact	Remarks
9k		From south	SUNART D.A.F.S., Estate Management Chesser House, Gorgie Road Edinburgh EH11 3AW		
9h		From north	FORESTRY COMMISSION 21 Church Street Inverness IN1 1EL	Lochaber Dorest District Torlundy, Fort William Tel: Fort William (0397) 2184	
9k	Ben Resipol	From south	SUNART (as above)		
9h		From north	FORESTRY COMMISSION (as above)		

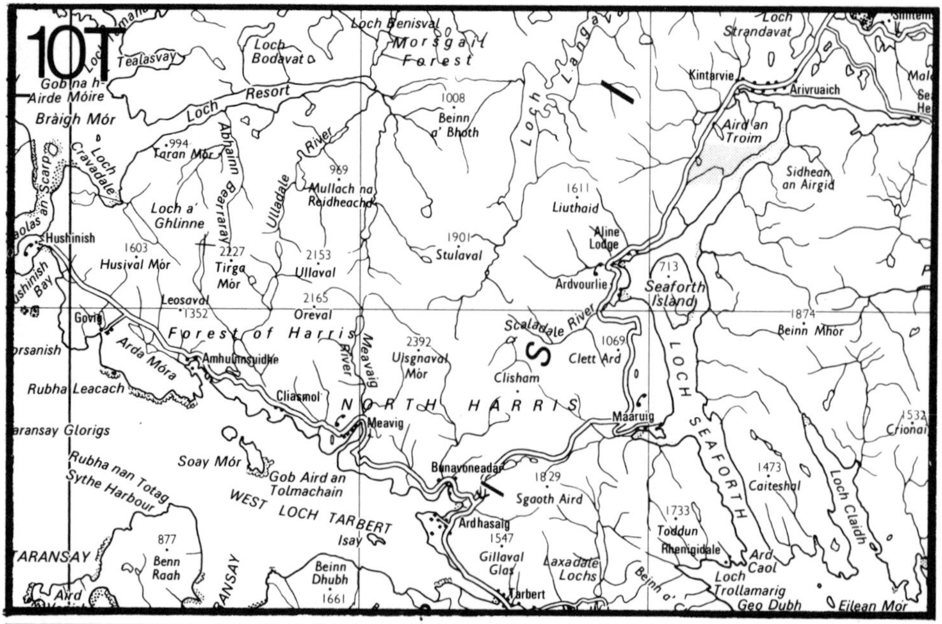
10T
Tealasvay
Gob na h-Airde Móire
Bràigh Mór
Loch Bodavat
Loch Benisval
Morsgail Forest
Loch Resort
Loch Langavat
Loch Strandavat
Kintarvie
Arivruaich
Aird an Troim
Sidhean an Airgid
994
Taran Mór
Abhainn Bearraray
Ulladale River
1008
Beinn a' Bhoth
969
Mullach na Reidheachd
Loch Cravadale
Loch a' Ghlinne
1611
Liuthaid
Hushinish
Hushinish Bay
1603
Husival Mór
2227
Tirga Mór
2153
Ullaval
1901
Stulaval
Aline Lodge
Ardvourlie
713
Seaforth Island
Leosaval
1352
2165
Oreval
Govig
Forest of Harris
Meavaig River
2392
Uisgnaval Mór
Scaladale River
1069
Clett Ard
1874
Beinn Mhór
Arda Móra
Amhuinnsuidhe
Rubha Leacach
Cliasmol
Clisham
NORTH HARRIS
Maaruig
LOCH SEAFORTH
Meavig
Soay Mór
Rubha nan Totag
Sythe Harbour
Gob Aird an Tolmachain
Bunavoneadar
1829
Sgaoth Aird
1473
Caiteshal
Loch Claidh
WEST LOCH TARBERT
Ardhasaig
1547
Gillaval Glas
1733
Toddun
Rhenigidale
Isay
877
Benn Raah
TARANSAY
Beinn Dhubh
1661
Laxadale Lochs
Ard Caol
Loch Trollamarig
Geo Dubh
Eilean Mór
Tarbert

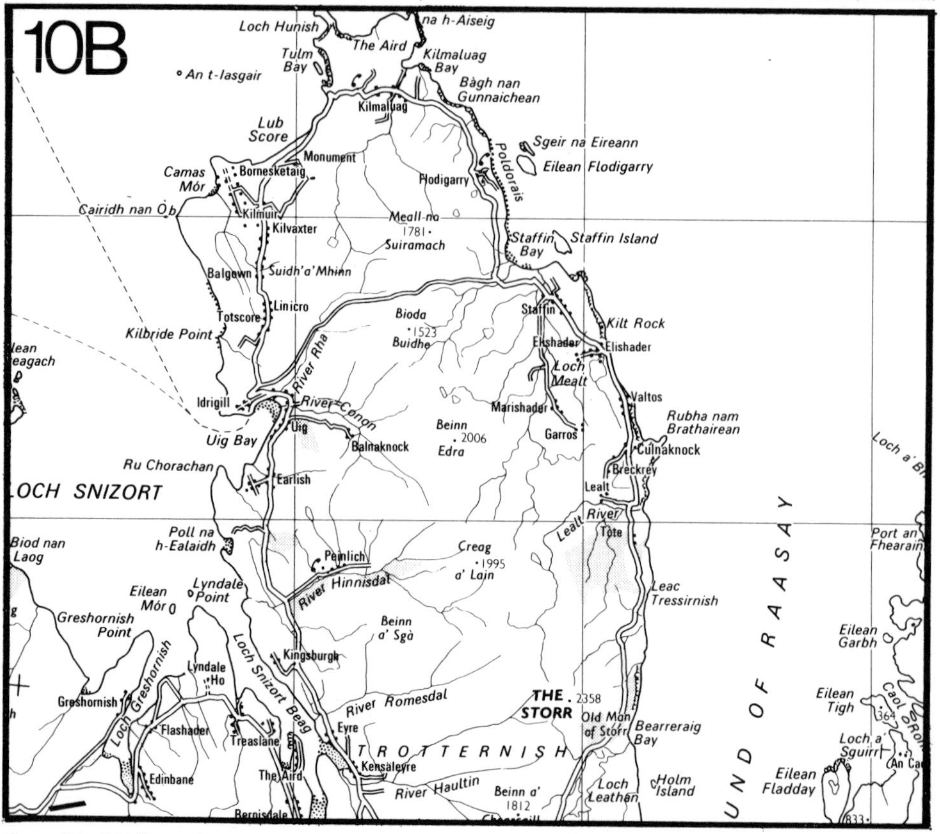
10B
Loch Hunish
The Aird
Tulm Bay
Kilmaluag Bay
An t-Iasgair
Bàgh nan Gunnaichean
Kilmaluag
Lub Score
Monument
Sgeir na Eireann
Eilean Flodigarry
Poldorais
Camas Mór
Bornesketaig
Flodigarry
Cairidh nan Ob
Kilmuir
Kilvaxter
Meall-na Suiramach
1781
Staffin Bay
Staffin Island
Balgown
Suidh'a'Mhinn
Totscore
Linicro
Bioda Buidhe
1523
Staffin
Kilt Rock
Kilbride Point
Elishader
Loch Mealt
River Rha
Valtos
Idrigill
River Conon
Marishader
Rubha nam Brathairean
Uig Bay
Uig
Beinn Edra
2006
Garros
Balnaknock
Culnaknock
Ru Chorachan
Breckrey
Earlish
Lealt
LOCH SNIZORT
Lealt River
Tote
Poll na h-Ealaidh
Biod nan Laog
Peinlich
Creag a' Lain
1995
River Hinnisdal
Leac Tressirnish
Eilean Mór
Lyndale Point
Greshornish Point
Beinn a' Sgà
Eilean Garbh
Loch Greshornish
Loch Snizort Beag
Kingsburgh
Lyndale Ho
THE STORR
2358
Eilean Tigh
Greshornish
River Romesdal
Old Man of Storr
Bearreraig Bay
Flashader
Treaslane
Eyre
TROTTERNISH
Edinbane
The Aird
Kensaleyre
River Haultin
Beinn a'
1812
Loch Leathan
Holm Island
Eilean Fladday
Loch a' Sguirr
SOUND OF RAASAY
Port an Fhearain
Caol Rona
833
364

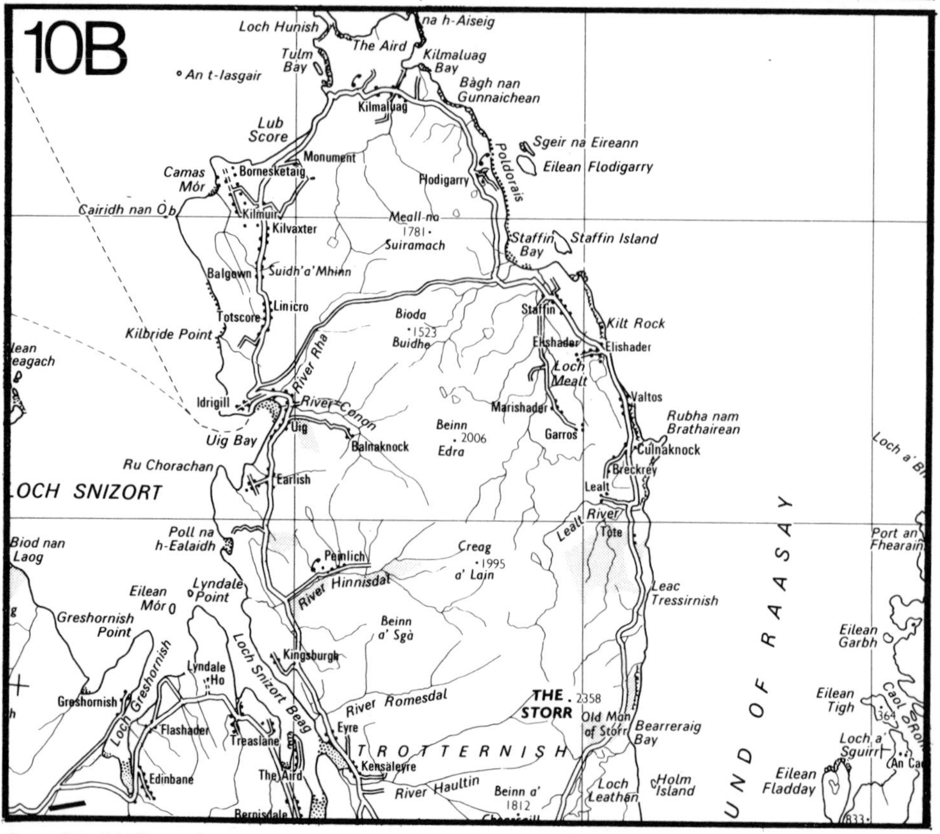

Map 10T — North Harris

References	Estate
10T/a	

Hills

Tirga Mor
Clisham
Beinn Mhor

Map 10B — Skye (Trotternish)

References	Estate
10B/a	TROTTERNISH & STORR
10B/b	FORESTRY COMMISSION

Hills

The Storr
Quirang

Map/Estate Reference	Mountain or Mountain Group	Approaches	Estate	Contact	Remarks
10T/a	Tirga Mhor Clisham Beinn Mhor				
10B/a	The Storr Quirang	From any public road throughout the area	D.A.F.S. Estate Mangement (A) Chesser House Gorgie Road, Edinburgh Edinburgh EH11 2AW	D.A.F.S. Estate Office Portree Skye, IV51 9DH Tel: Portree (0478) 2516	
10B/b			FORESTRY COMMISSION 231 Corstorphine Road Edinburgh EH12 7AT	Wester Ross Forest District Balmacara, Ross-shire Tel: Balmacara (059 986) 321	Follow the main road north from the Forestry Commission car park then follow the fence line along the northern boundary of the F.C. block

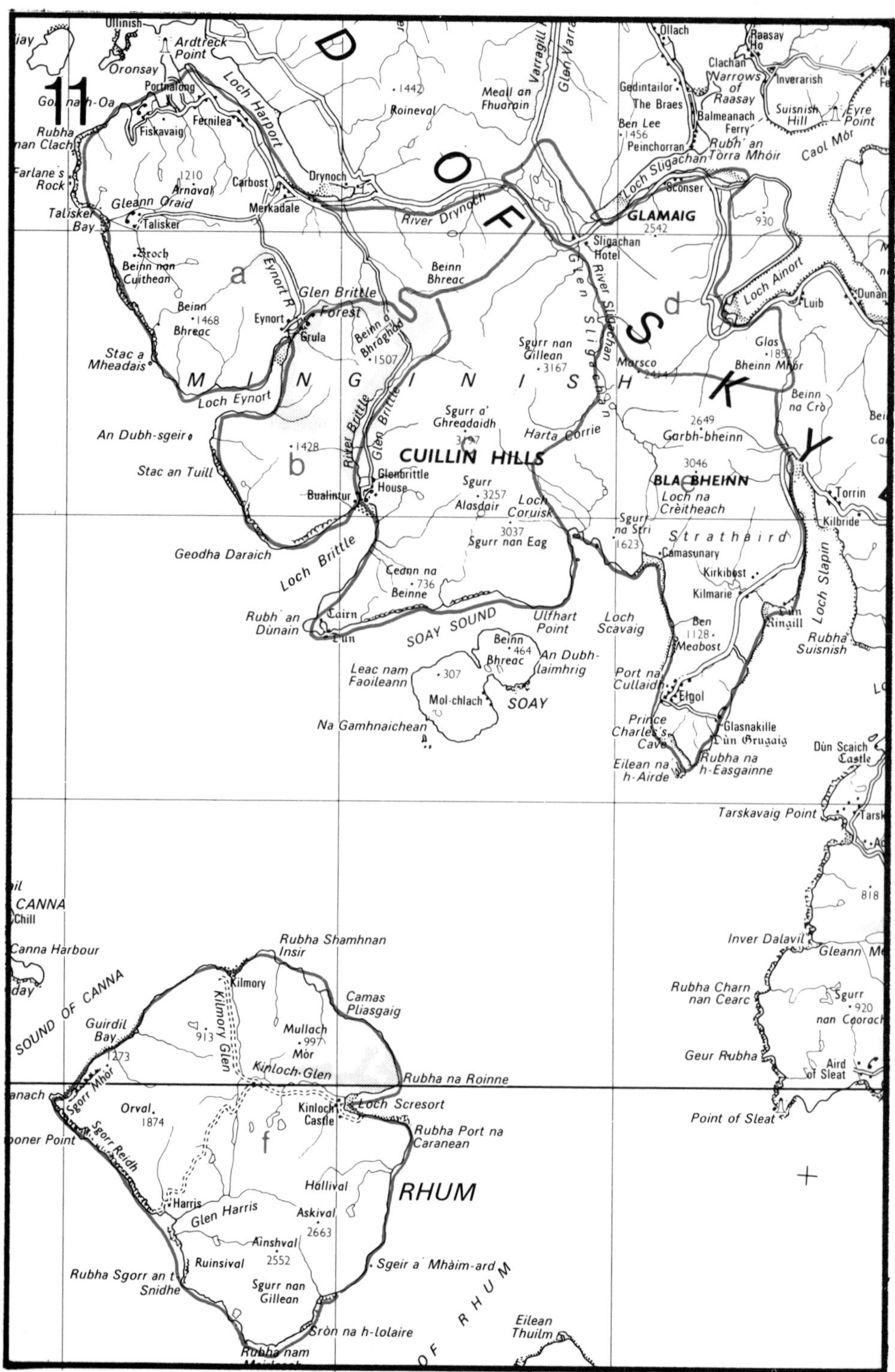
11
Ullinish
Ardtreck Point
Oronsay
Portnalong
Fiskavaig
Fernilea
Rubha
Farlane's Rock
Talisker Bay
Talisker
Gleann Oraid
1210
Arnaval
Carbost
Merkadale
Drynoch
Loch Harport
River Drynoch
·1442
Roineval
Meall an Fhuarain
Varragill
Glen Varragill
Broch
Beinn nan Cuithean
a
Eynort R
Beinn ·1468 Bhreac
Eynort
Glen Brittle
Forest
Grula
Beinn a' Bhràghad
·1507
Stac a Mheadais
M I N G I N I S H
Loch Eynort
An Dubh-sgeir
·1428
b
Stac an Tuill
River Brittle
Glen Brittle
Glenbrittle House
Bualintur
Geodha Daraich
Loch Brittle
Beinn Bhreac
D O F S K Y
Ollach
Raasay Ho
Clachan
Narrows of Raasay
Inverarish
Gedintailor
The Braes
Balmeanach
Suisnish Hill
Eyre Point
Ben Lee ·1456
Peinchorran
Ferry
Rubh' an Torra Mhóir
Caol Mór
Loch Sligachan
Sconser
GLAMAIG
2542
930
Sligachan Hotel
Glen Sligachan
River Sligachan
Loch Ainort
Luib
d
Sgurr nan Gillean ·3167
Marsco
2414
Glas Bheinn Mhòr
·1852
Beinn na Crò
Sgurr a' Ghreadaidh
3197
Harta Corrie
CUILLIN HILLS
2649
Garbh-bheinn
3046
BLÀ BHEINN
Loch na Crèitheach
Sgurr ·3257 Alasdair
Loch Coruisk
3037
Sgurr nan Eag
Sgurr na Stri
1623
Strathaird
Camasunary
Kirkibost
Kilmarie
Torrin
Kilbride
Loch Slapin
Ceann na ·736 Beinne
Cairn
Rubh' an Dùnain
Dùn
SOAY SOUND
Ulfhart Point
Loch Scavaig
Ben 1128 Meabost
Dùn Ringill
Rubha Suisnish
Beinn ·464 Bhreac
An Dubh-laimhrig
Leac nam Faoileann
·307
Mol-chlach
SOAY
Na Gamhnaichean
Port na Cullaidh
Elgol
Prince Charles's Cave
Glasnakille
Dùn Grugaig
Eilean na h-Airde
Rubha na h-Easgainne
Dùn Scaich Castle
Tarskavaig Point
818
CANNA
Chill
Canna Harbour
SOUND OF CANNA
Rubha Shamhnan Insir
Kilmory
Camas Pliasgaig
Guirdil Bay
913
Kilmory Glen
Mullach ·997 Mór
273
Kinloch Glen
Rubha na Roinne
Sgorr Mhòr
Orval 1874
Kinloch Castle
Loch Scresort
Rubha Port na Caranean
Sgorr Reidh
f
Hallival
RHUM
Harris
Glen Harris
Askival 2663
Ainshval 2552
Ruinsival
Sgeir a' Mhàim-ard
Rubha Sgorr an t-Snidhe
Sgurr nan Gillean
Sròn na h-Iolaire
Eilean Thuilm
Rubha nam
OF RHUM
Inver Dalavil
Gleann
Rubha Charn nan Cearc
Sgurr ·920 nan Caorach
Geur Rubha
Aird of Sleat
Point of Sleat

Map 11 — Skye and Rhum Cuillins

Reference	Estate Name
11a	MACLEOD
11b	FORESTRY COMMISSION
11c	DUNVEGAN
11d	SCONSER
11e	STRATHAIRD
11f	RHUM

Hills

Glamaig
Black Cuillin
Red Cuillin
Bla Bheinn
Island of Rhum

Map/Estate Reference	Mountain or Mountain Group	Approaches	Estate	Contact	Remarks
11d	Glamaig (Sligachan)	All routes	SCONSER Central Skye Hotels Ltd Sligachan Hotel Skye	Ian S. Campbell Sligachan Tel: Sligachan (047 852) 232	Camping permitted.
11a	Black Cuillin	All routes	MACLEOD ESTATE John Macleod of Macleod Dunvegan Skye	Gideon MacRae Glenbrittle Tel: Carbost (047 842) 232	Camping on authorised campsite. BMC/MCofS hut.
11b		From south	FORESTRY COMMISSION 231 Corstorphine Road EDINBURGH EH12 7AT	Wester Ross Forest District Balmacara, Ross-shire Tel: Balmacara (059 986) 321	
11d	Red Cuillin Bla Bheinn	From north	SCONSER (as above)	Ian S.Campbell (as above)	
11c		From west	DUNVEGAN John Macleod of Macleod (as above)		
11e		Loch Slapin	STRATHAIRD Broadford Skye	The Manager Tel: Loch Scavaig (047 16) 232	

11b		From east	FORESTRY COMMISSION (as above)	(as above)	
11f	Rhum	All routes	RHUM Nature Conservancy Council Fraser Darling House Culduthel Road Inverness	Chief Warden Isle of Rhum Tel: Mallaig (0687) 2026	Prior permission essential to visit Rhum. Various parts of the island may be closed at certain times of the year.

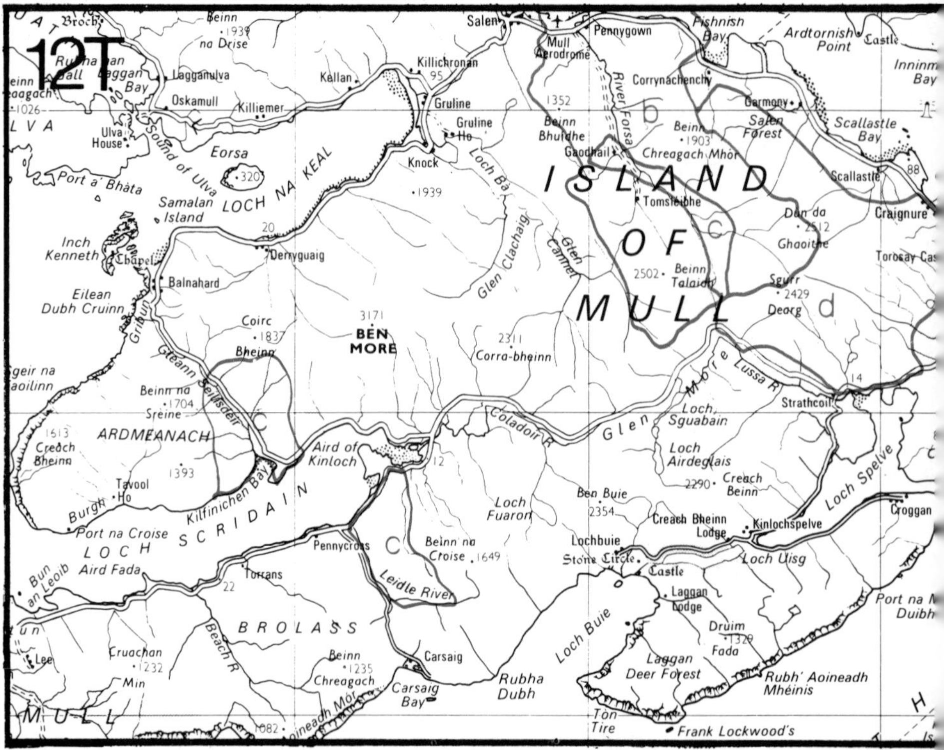
12T
Salen
Pennygown
Fishnish Bay
Ardtornish Point
Castle
Inninmore Bay
Mull Aerodrome
Beinn na Drise
1939
Rubha nan Gall
Laggan Bay
Lagganulva
Kellan
Killichronan
95
Corrynachenchy
Garmony
Oskamull
Killiemer
Gruline
Gruline Ho
Ulva House
Sound of Ulva
Eorsa
320
LOCH NA KEAL
Knock
Loch Bà
River Forsa
1352
Beinn Bhuidhe
Gaodhail
Beinn Chreagach Mhòr
1903
Salen Forest
Scallastle Bay
Scallastle
88
Port a' Bhàta
Samalan Island
ISLAND OF MULL
Tomsléibhe
Dùn da Ghaoithe
2512
Craignure
Inch Kenneth
Chapel
20
Derryguaig
Glen Clachaig
Glen Cannel
2502
Beinn Talaidh
Torosay Castle
Balnahard
Sgurr Dearg
2429
Eilean Dubh Cruinn
Gribun
Coirc Bheinn
1837
3171
BEN MORE
2311
Corra-bheinn
Gleann Seilisdeir
Beinn na Sreine
1704
Lussa R
Strathcoil
14
Glen Mòre
Coladoir R
Loch Sguabain
ARDMEANACH
1613
Creach Bheinn
1393
Aird of Kinloch
12
Loch Airdeglais
Loch Spelve
Tavool Ho
Burgh
Kilfinichen Bay
LOCH SCRIDAIN
Loch Fuaron
Ben Buie
2354
2290
Creach Beinn
Croggan
Creach Bheinn Lodge
Kinlochspelve
Port na Croise
Pennycross
Beinn na Croise
1649
Lochbuie
Stone Circle
Castle
Loch Uisg
Aird Fada
Bun an Leoib
Torrans
22
Leidle River
Laggan Lodge
Port na Muice Duibhe
BROLASS
Loch Buie
Druim Fada
1329
Lee
Cruachan Min
1232
Beach R
Beinn Chreagach
1235
Carsaig
Carsaig Bay
Rubha Dubh
Laggan Deer Forest
Rubh' Aoineadh Mhéinis
MULL
1082
Aoineadh Mòr
Tòn Tire
Frank Lockwood's

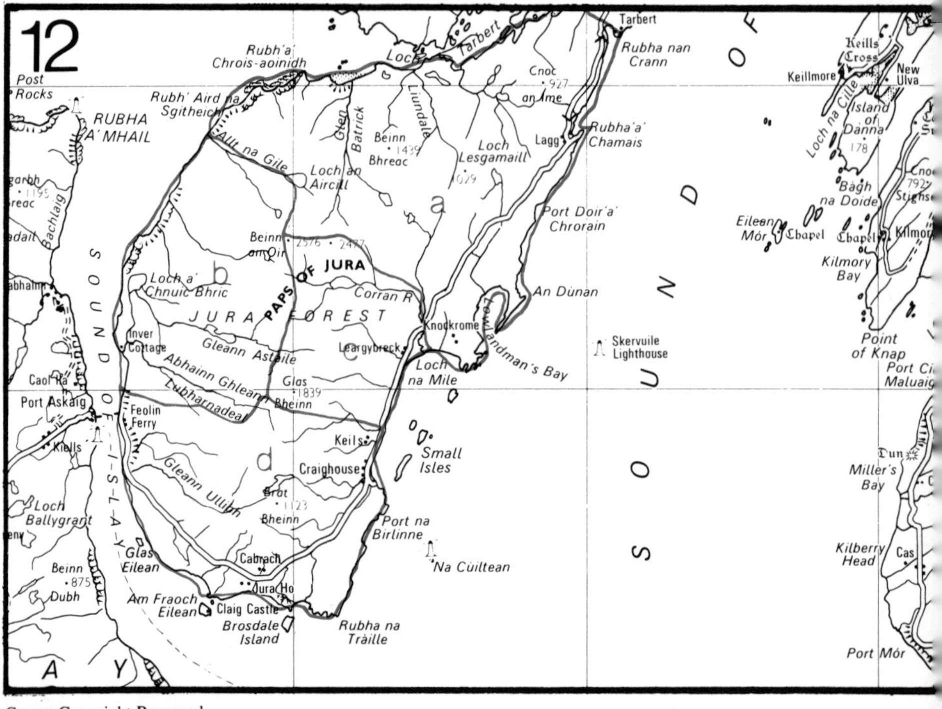
12
Tarbert
Rubh'a' Chrois-aoinidh
Loch Tarbert
Rubha nan Crann
Post Rocks
Rubh' Aird na Sgitheich
Cnoc an Ime
927
Keills Cross
Keillmore
New Ulva
RUBHA A' MHAIL
Glen Batrick
Liundale
Beinn Bhreac
1439
Lagg
Rubha'a' Chamais
Loch na Cille
Island of Danna
178
Allt na Gile
Loch an Aircill
Loch Lesgamaill
1029
Bàgh na Doide
Port Doir'a' Chrorain
Eilean Mór
Chapel
Chapel
Kilmory
Beinn an Oir
2576
2477
Kilmory Bay
Loch a' Chnuic Bhric
PAPS OF JURA
Corran R
An Dùnan
JURA FOREST
SOUND OF JURA
Knockrome
Lowlandman's Bay
Inver Cottage
Gleann Astaile
Leargybreck
Skervuile Lighthouse
Point of Knap
Abhainn Ghleann
Loch na Mile
Port Cill Maluaig
Caol Ila
Glas Bheinn
1839
Port Askaig
Lùbharnadeal
Feolin Ferry
Kiells
Keils
Small Isles
Dun
Miller's Bay
Craighouse
Gleann Ullibh
Loch Ballygrant
Brat Bheinn
1123
SOUND OF ISLAY
Port na Birlinne
Na Cùiltean
Kilberry Head
Glas Eilean
Cabrach
Beinn Dubh
875
Jura Ho
Am Fraoch Eilean
Claig Castle
Brosdale Island
Rubha na Tràille
Port Mór

Map 12T — Mull

Reference	Estate Name
12T/a	KNOCK
12T/b	GLENFORSA
12T/c	FORESTRY COMMISSION
12T/d	TOROSAY
12T/e	LOCHBUIE

Hills

Glen Forsa
Beinn Bhuidhe
Beinn Talaidh
Dun da Gaoithe
Sgurr Dearg
Ben More
Corra-bheinn
Ben Buie
Creach Beinn

Map 12B — South Jura

Reference	Estate Name
12B/a	TARBERT
12B/b	INVER
12B/c	FOREST
12B/d	ARDFIN

Hills

Paps of Jura

Map/Estate Reference	Mountain or Mountain Group	Approaches	Estate	Contact	Remarks
12T/b	Glen Forsa Beinn Bhuidhe Beinn Talaidh Dun da Gaoithe Sgurr Dearg	All routes	GLENFORSA D.A.F.S. Estate Management (H) Chesser House Gorgie Road Edinburgh EH11 3AW	D.A.F.S. Oban Tel: Oban (0631) 63071 or Mr Gillivray, at Pennygowan Tel: Aros (068 03) 335 or Mr MacPhail at Callachally Tel: Aros (068 03) 424	
12T/d		From east	TOROSAY Mr C James Torosay, Craignure PA65 6AY	Estate Office Craignure Tel: Craignure (068 02) 421	In winter months please leave word at Estate Office. Preferred route via Television Mast Road.
12T/a	Ben More Corra-Bheinn	Loch na Keal	KNOCK	Tel: Aros (068 03) 410	
12T/e	Ben Buie Creach Beinn		LOCHBUIE		
12T/c			FORESTRY COMMISSION 21 Church Street Inverness IV1 1EL	Mull Forest District Aros, Isle of Mull Tel:Aros(068 03) 346	

12B/a	Paps of Jura	All routes	TARBERT The Viscount Astor Ginge Manor Wantage OXON OX12 8QT	Neil MacInnes Gatehouse Graighouse, Isle of Jura Argyll Tel: Jura (049 682) 207
12B/b			INVER Mr William Lithgow	Stalker Donald Darroch Tel: Jura (049 682)223
12B/c			FOREST Lord Vesty	Head Stalker Ian Cameron Tel: Jura (049 682) 230
12B/d			ARDFIN Mr Riley-Smtih	Head Stalker William Macdonald Tel: Jura (049 682) 396

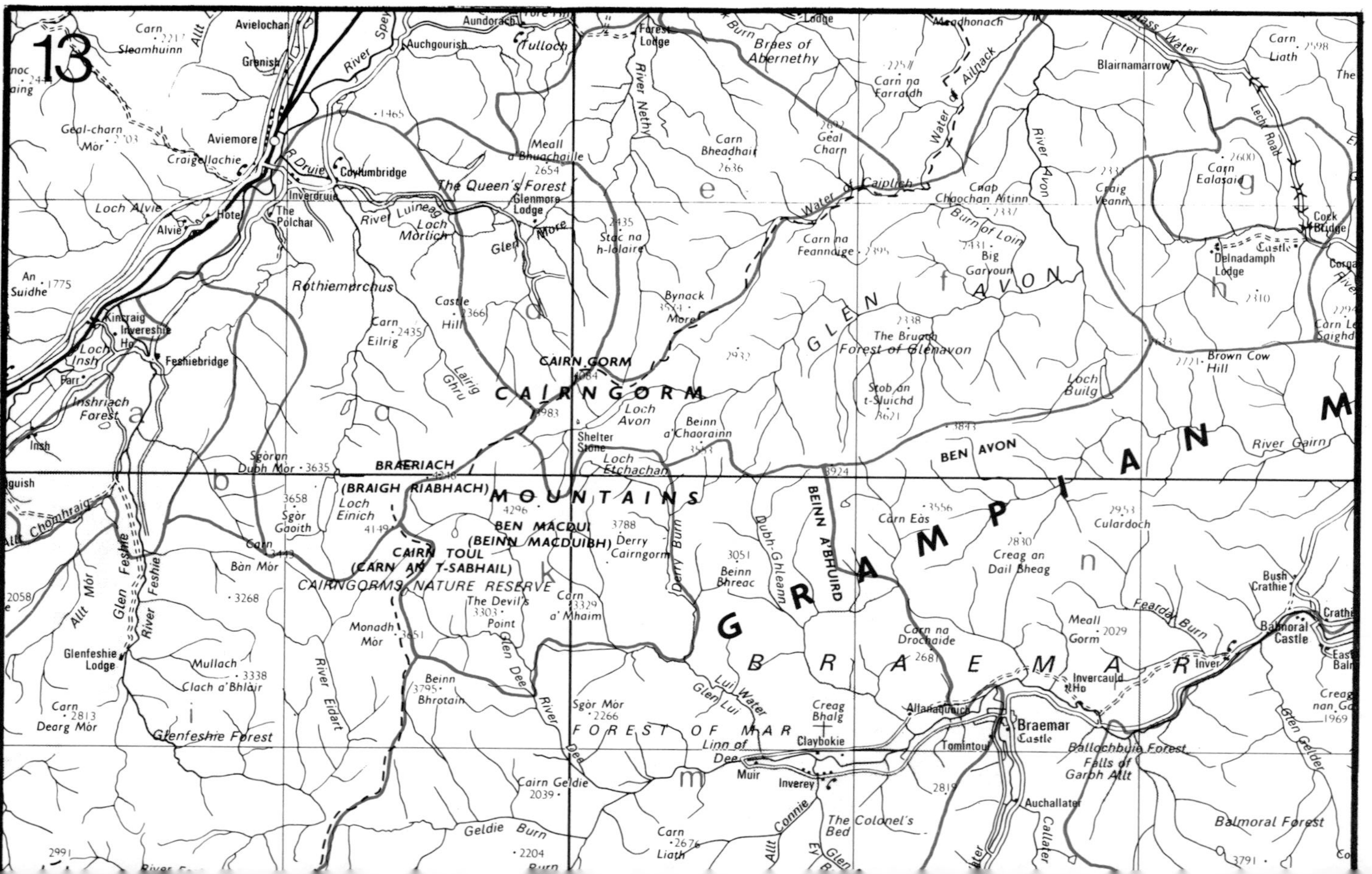
13
GRAMPIAN MOUNTAINS
CAIRNGORM
CAIRN GORM
BEN MACDUI (BEINN MACDUIBH)
CAIRN TOUL (CARN AN T-SABHAIL)
BRAERIACH (BRAIGH RIABHACH)
BEINN A'BHUIRD
BEN AVON
GLEN AVON
FOREST OF MAR
BRAEMAR
CAIRNGORMS NATURE RESERVE
Aviemore
Coylumbridge
Inverdruie
Glenmore Lodge
The Queen's Forest
Loch Morlich
Rothiemurchus
Lairig Ghru
Loch Avon
Shelter Stone
Loch Etchachan
Derry Cairngorm
Derry Burn
Glen Lui
Lui Water
Linn of Dee
River Dee
Glen Dee
The Devil's Point
Braemar
Braemar Castle
Balmoral Castle
Balmoral Forest
Inverey
Claybokie
Allanaquoich
Invercauld Ho
Ballochbuie Forest
Falls of Garbh Allt
Auchallater
Callater
Crathie
Glen Gelder
Feardar Burn
Culardoch
Creag an Dail Bheag
Carn Eas
Carn na Drochaide
Beinn Bhreac
Dubh-Ghleann
Beinn a'Chaorainn
Bynack More
Stac na h-Iolaire
Forest Lodge
River Nethy
Braes of Abernethy
Carn Bheadhair
Water of Caiplich
Water of Ailnack
River Avon
Loch Builg
Brown Cow Hill
Delnadamph Lodge
Carn Ealasaid
Lecht Road
Cock Bridge
Blairnamarrow
Tomintoul
Glenfeshie Lodge
Glen Feshie
River Feshie
Glenfeshie Forest
Mullach Clach a'Bhlair
River Eidart
Monadh Mòr
Beinn Bhrotain
Sgòr Gaoith
Loch Einich
Feshiebridge
Kincraig
Loch Insh
Insh
Inshriach Forest
Loch Alvie
Alvie
Craigellachie
Geal-charn Mòr
River Spey
Aundorach
Auchgourish
Tulloch
Carn Eilrig
Castle Hill
Meall a'Bhuachaille
Sgòr Mòr
Cairn Geldie
Geldie Burn
Carn Dearg Mòr
Big Garvoun
Allt Connie
The Colonel's Bed

Map 13 — Cairngorms

Reference	Estate Name
13a	FORESTRY COMMISSION
13b	INVERESHIE
13c	ROTHIEMURCHUS
13d	GLEN MORE
13e	ABERNETHY FOREST LODGE
13f	GLENAVON
13g	ALLARGLE
13h	DALNADAMPH
13i	GLENFESHIE
13k	DERRY CAIRNGORM
13m	MAR LODGE
13n	INVERCAULD

Hills

Braeriach
Lairig Ghru
Cairn Gorm
Bynack More
Ben Avon
Beinn a' Bhuird
Glenfeshie Hills
Beinn Bhrotain
Cairn Toul
Ben Macdui
Derry Cairngorm
Beinn a' Chaorainn
Sgor Gaoith

Map/Estate Reference	Mountain or Mountain Group	Approaches	Estate	Contact	Remarks
13c	Braeriach Lairig Ghru	Colyumbridge Glen Einich	ROTHIEMURCHUS John Grant of Rothiemurchus Rothiemurchus Estate Office by Aviemore PH22 1QH	Countryside Ranger Service Aviemore Tel: Aviemore (0479) 810858	Collect or send for free footpath map
13d		From north-east	GLEN MORE		
13b		From west	INVERESHIE Nature Conservancy Council 17 Rubislaw Terrace Aberdeen AB1 1XE	David Gowans Head Warden, Achantoul Aviemore Tel Aviemore (0479) 810477	See roadsign maps for parking
13e	Cairn Gorm Bynack More	Strath Nethy	ABERNETHY FOREST LODGE Messrs R.C. & D.M. Naylor Birch Lane House, Flaunden Nr. Hemel Hempstead, Herts	Mr C. Robertson Forest Lodge, Nethy Bridge Tel: Nethy Bridge (047 982) 619	
13f			GLENAVON (Inchrory) INCHRORY LODGE D.S. Wills, Tomintoul Banffshire AB3 9HX	Tel: Tomintoul (080 74) 256	

13m		From south	MAR LODGE Harlow & Jones (Investments) Ltd Mar Lodge Braemar	Mrs S. Dempster Mar Lodge Tel: Braemar (033 83) 216 or Mr W. Forbes Tel: Braemar (033 833) 676	
13c	Beinn Bhrotain Cairn Toul Ben Macdui Derry Cairgorm Beinn a' Chaorainn	From north	ROTHIEMURCHUS John Grant of Rothiemurchus Rothiemurchus Estate Office by Aviemore PH22 1QH	Countryside Ranger Service Aviemore Tel: Aviemore (0479) 810858	Collect or send for free footpath map.
13d			GLEN MORE		
13e			ABERNETHY FOREST LODGE Messrs R.C. & D.M. Naylor Birch Lane House, Flaunden Nr. Hemel Hempstead Herts	Mr C. Robertson Forest Lodge Nethy Bridge Tel: Nethy Bridge (047 982) 619	
13f		From north and east	GLENAVON (Inchrory) INCHRORY LODGE D.S. Wills Tomintoul Ballindalloch Banffshire AB3 9HX	Tel: Tomintoul (080 74) 256	

Map/Estate Reference	Mountain or Mountain Group	Approaches	Estate	Contact	Remarks
13k			CAIRNGORM NATIONAL NATURE RESERVE Nature Conservancy Council 17 Rubislaw Terrace Aberdeen	David Gowans Head Warden Achantoul Tel: Aviemore (0479) 810477	
13f	Ben Avon Beinn a' Bhuird	Glen Avon	GLEN AVON (Inchrory) INCHRORY LODGE D.S. Wills Tomintoul, Ballindalloch Banffshire AB3 9HX	Tel: Tomintoul (080 74) 256	
13n		Gleann an t-Slugain and Glen Gairn	INVERCAULD Capt. A.A.C. Farquharson, MC per Factor Invercauld Estate Office Braemar	Derek P. Petrie Factor Tel: Braemar (033 83) 224 or P. Fraser Head Stalker Tel: Braemar (033 83) 267	For Gleann an t-Slugain park in the area of the Keiloch. For Glen Cairn park just off the B976.
13h		From north-east	DELNADAMPH The Balmoral Estates' Trustees Balmoral Estate Office Balmoral, Ballater Aberdeenshire		

13g			ALLARGLE		
13k		All routes	CAIRNGORM NATIONAL NATURE RESERVE Nature Conservancy Council 17 Rubislaw Terrace Aberdeen	David Gowans Head Warden Achantoul, Aviemore Tel: Aviemore (0479) 810477	
13i		From south-west	GLENFESHIE West Highland Woodlands The Estate Office Batsford Moreton-in -Marsh Glos. GL56 9QF	A. Dempster Head Stalker Glenfeshie Estate Kincraig Tel: Kingussie (054 02) 453	Bothy at Ruigh Aiteachun No cutting of live timber please.
13m		From south-east	MAR LODGE Harlow & Jones (Investments) Ltd Mar Lodge Braemar	Mrs. S. Dempster Mar Lodge Tel: Braemar (033 83) 216 or Mr W. Forbes Tel: Braemar (033 83) 676	
13i	Sgor Gaoith and Glenfeshie Hills	Glen Feshie	GLENFESHIE (as above)	A. Dempster (as above)	
13a		From Feshiebridge	FORESTRY COMMISSION 21 Church Street Inverness IV1 1EL	Inverness Forest Distrct Smithton, Inverness Tel: Inverness (0463) 791575	

Map/Estate Reference	Mountain or Mountain Group	Approaches	Estate	Contact	Remarks
13b			INVERESHIE Nature Conservancy Council 17 Rubislaw Terrace Aberdeen AB1 1XE	David Gowans Head Warden Achantoul, Aviemore Tel: Aviemore (0479) 810477	See roadsign maps for parking.

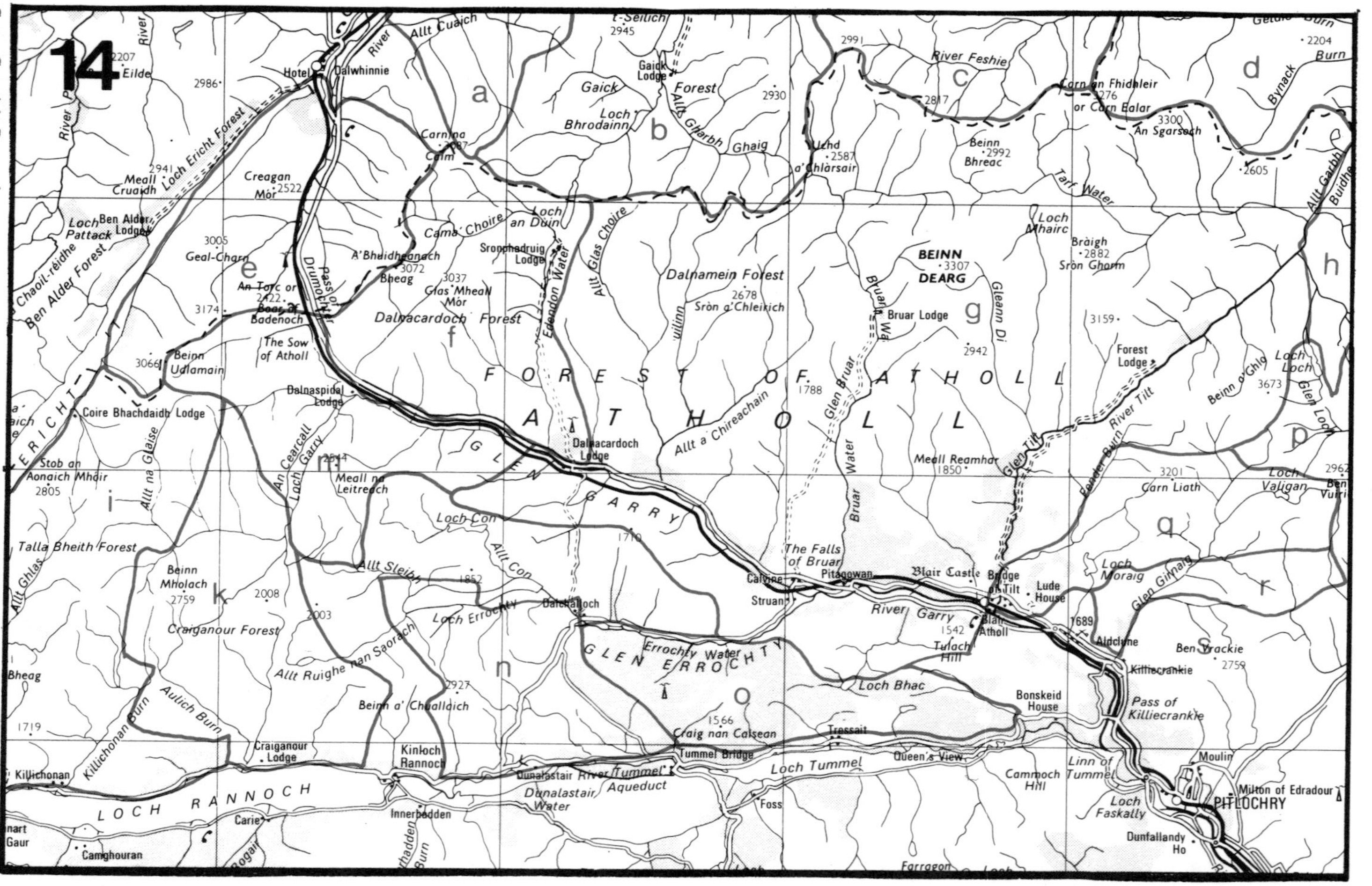

Crown Copyright Reserved

Map 14 — Drumochter — Glen Tilt

Reference	Estate Name
14a	ETTERIDGE & PHONES
14b	GAICK
14c	GLENFESHIE
14d	MAR LODGE
14e	DRUMOCHTER
14f	DALNACARDOCH
14g	ATHOLL
14h	FEALAR
14i	TALLADH-BEITH
14k	CRAIGANOUR
14m	DALNASPIDAL
14n	DUNALASTAIR
14o	FORESTRY COMMISSION
14p	GLENFERNATE
14q	LUDE
14r	URRARD
14s	BALEDMUND

Hills

Meall Chuaich
Carn na Caim
A'Bhuidheanach Bheag
An Sgarsoch
Carn Ealar
Beinn Dearg
Carn a' Chlamain
Beinn a' Ghlo
Ben Molach
Ben Vrackie

Map/Estate Reference	Mountain or Mountain Group	Approaches	Estate	Contact	Remarks
14a	Meall Chuaich	A9 and Loch Cuaich	ETTERIDGE & PHONES The Hon P. Samuel Phones Lodge, Newtonmore	Tel: Dalwhinnie (052 82) 254	
14b		Glen Tromie	GAICK Gaick Estates Ltd Gaick Lodge, Kingussie	Tel: Kingussie (054 02) 682	
14e	Carn na Caim A. Bhuidheanach Bheag	From west and south- west	*NORTH AND SOUTH DRUMOCHTER Mrs J. Drysdale Kilrie Kirkcaldy, Fife	Mr A. Anderson North Drumtochter Lodge Dalwhinnie Tel: Dalwhinnie (052 82) 209	
14f		From south	DALNACARDOCH The Duke of Atholl per A.W. Barbour, FRICS Atholl Estates Office Blair Atholl, Perthshire	Tel: Comrie (0764) 553	
14a		From north and north -east	ETTERIDGE & PHONES (as above)	(as above)	
14b			GAICK (as above)	(as above)	

*East Loch Ericht Deer Management Group Member

14c	An Sgarsoch Carn Ealar	Glen Feshie	GLENFESHIE West Highland Woodlands The Estate Office Batsford, Moreton-in-Marsh Glos. GL56 9QF	A.Dempster Head Stalker Glenfeshie Estate, Kincraig Tel: Kingussie (054 02) 453	Bothy at Ruigh Aiteachun. No cutting of live timber please.
14d		From north-east (Linn of Dee)	MAR LODGE Harlow & Jones (Investments) Ltd Mar Lodge Braemar	Mrs S. Dempster Mar Lodge Tel: Braemar (033 83) 216 or Mr W. Forbes Tel: Braemar (033 83) 676	
14g		From south (Blair Atholl)	ATHOLL The Duke of Atholl per A.W. Barbour, FRICS Atholl Estate Office Blair Atholl, Perthshire	The Factor Atholl Estates Office Tel: Blair Atholl (079 681) 355	Some camping allowed with permission. Vehicle access to Glen Tilt permitted - charge of £2 per car.
14g	Beinn Dearg Carn a' Chlamain Beinn a' Ghlo	Old Blair and Glen Tilt	ATHOLL (as above)	The Factor (as above)	
14q		Glen Fender	LUDE Major Gordon Lude Farm Blair Atholl Perthshire	Tel: Blair Atholl (079 681) 240	

Map/Estate Reference	Mountain or Mountain Group	Approaches	Estate	Contact	Remarks
14p		From east (Glenfernate road or path from Glen Tilt)	FEALAR Spearman Trustees per Atholl Estates Estates Office, Blair Atholl Perthshire	The Factor Atholl Estates Office Tel: Blair Atholl (079 681) 355	Camping by arrangment with Factor only. No cars.
14p		Glenfernate	GLENFERNATE David Heathcote Amory Glenfernate Enochdu Perthshire	Gordon MacGregor Glenfernate Tel: Strathardle (025 081) 205	Parking at public road available. No cars beyond PRIVATE sign. Dogs on lead. Beware stalking August to February.
14m	Ben Mholach	From north	*DALNASPIDAL B.R. Adams Dalnaspidal Lodge Calvine by Pitlochry, Perthshire	John Kennedy Stalker Old Schoolhouse, Dalnaspidal Tel: Calvine (079 683)204	Parking at Dalnaspidal Station or in lay-by on A9.
14i		From south and south-east	*TALLADH-a-BHEITHE per Strathtay Estate Office Boltachan by Aberfeldy Perthshire	J.T. Boscawen Strathtay Estate Office Bolachan by Aberfeldy Tel: Aberfeldy (0887) 20496	

* East Loch Ericht Deer Management Group Member

14k			*CRAIGANOUR Astel Ltd per Strathtay Estate Office Bolachan by Aberfeldy, Perthshire	H. Littlejohn Craiganour Lodge Rannoch Station Tel: Kinloch Rannoch (088 22) 324	
14n		From Kinloch Rannoch	*DUNALASTAIR Capt. de Sales la Terriere 13 Clarendon Cres. Edinburgh	D. Dunlop Tel: Kinloch Rannoch (088 22) 305	
14s	Ben Vrackie	From A9	BALEDMUND A.F. Ferguson Old Faskally farm Killiecrankie Pitlochry, Perthshire	J.L.F. Ferguson Baledmund Estate Office Pitfourie, Pitlochry Tel: Pitlochry (0796) 2721	Use sign-posted car park. Keep dogs on lead or to heel.
14r		Glen Girnaig	URRARD Urrard Estate Co. Ltd Urrard, Killiecrankie Pitlochry Perthshire PH16 5LN		

*East Loch Ericht Deer Management Group Member

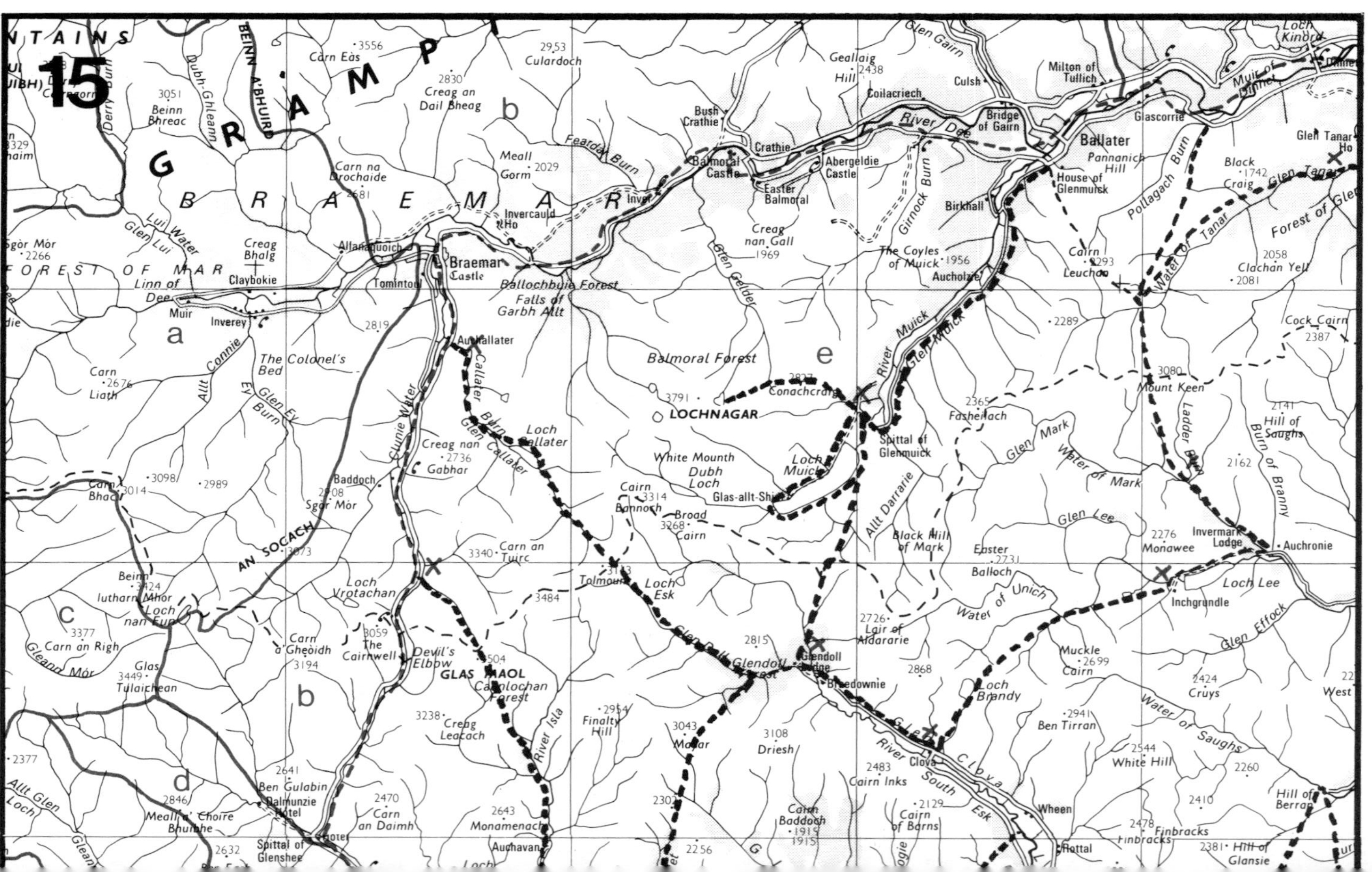
15
Ballater
Braemar
Castle
LOCHNAGAR
Balmoral Forest
Balmoral Castle
Crathie
Abergeldie Castle
River Dee
Glen Gelder
Loch Muick
Spittal of Glenmuick
River Muick
Dubh Loch
White Mounth
Glas-allt-Shiel
Loch Callater
Callater Burn
Glen Callater
Auchallater
Clunie Water
GLAS MAOL
Caenlochan Forest
The Cairnwell
Devil's Elbow
Loch Vrotachan
Carn a' Gheoidh
Spittal of Glenshee
Glen Ey
Ey Burn
The Colonel's Bed
Inverey
Linn of Dee
Claybokie
Creag Bhalg
BEINN A' BHUIRD
Dubh-Ghleann
Beinn Bhreac
Glen Lui
Lui Water
Allanaquoich
Invercauld Ho
Falls of Garbh Allt
Ballochbuie Forest
Feardar Burn
Meall Gorm
Culardoch
Creag an Dail Bheag
Carn Eàs
Carn na Drochaide
Geallaig Hill
Coilacriech
Bridge of Gairn
Glen Gairn
Culsh
Milton of Tullich
Pannanich Hill
House of Glenmuick
Birkhall
The Coyles of Muick
Girnock Burn
Glascorrie
Pollagach Burn
Water of Tanar
Glen Tanar Ho
Forest of Glen Tanar
Black Craig
Clachan Yell
Cock Cairn
Mount Keen
Hill of Saughs
Burn of Branny
Auchronie
Invermark Lodge
Loch Lee
Glen Effock
Inchgrundle
Monawee
Ladder Burn
Water of Mark
Glen Mark
Glen Lee
Fasheilach
Conachcraig
Black Hill of Mark
Allt Darrarie
Lair of Aldararie
Easter Balloch
Water of Unich
Loch Brandy
Muckle Cairn
Cruys
Water of Saughs
White Hill
Ben Tirran
Hill of Glansie
Finbracks
Wheen
Glen Clova
River Clova
South Esk
Cairn of Barns
Cairn Inks
Braedownie
Glendoll Lodge
Glendoll Forest
Driesh
Cairn Baddoch
Mayar
Loch Esk
Tolmount
Broad Cairn
Cairn Bannoch
Finalty Hill
River Isla
Creag Leacach
Carn an Tuirc
Monamenach
Auchavan
Carn an Daimh
Ben Gulabin
Dalmunzie Hotel
Meall a' Choire Bhuidhe
Glas Tulaichean
Carn an Righ
Gleann Mór
Beinn Iutharn Mhor
Loch nan Eun
Carn Bhac
Carn Liath
Sgòr Mór
AN SOCACH
Sgor Mór
Baddoch
Creag nan Gabhar
Allt Glen Loch
Allt Connie
F O R E S T O F M A R
G R A M P
B R A E M A R

Map 15 — Glenshee — Lochnagar

Reference	Estate Name
15a	MAR LODGE
15b	INVERCAULD (Area outside East Grampian Deer Management Group Area)
15c	FEALAR
15d	DALMUNZIE
15e	EAST GRAMPIAN DEER MANAGEMENT GROUP AREA (The following estates are listed in the text according to the approaches used) INVERCAULD BALMORAL AIRLIE GLEN TANAR GLENMUICK DALHOUSIE TULCHAN GLENPROSEN

Hills

Lochnagar
Broad Cairn Group
Mount Keen
An Socach
Glas Tulaichean
Carn Bhac
The Cairnwell
Carn an t-Sagairt Mor
Tolmount
Glas Maol
Cairn of Claise
Driesh
Mayar
Ben Tirran

The boundary for the East Grampian Deer Management Group area is marked on the map as a broken red line.
The recognised hill tracks within the area are marked on the map as broken black lines. Locations of access notices are marked on the map with a red cross.

Map/Estate Reference	Mountain or Mountain Group	Approaches	Estate	Contact	Remarks
15a	An Socach Glas Tulaichean Carn Bhac The Cairnwell	Glen Ey	MAR LODGE Harlow & Jones (Investments) Ltd Mar Lodge Braemar	Mrs S. Dempster Mar Lodge Tel: Braemar (033 83) 216 or Mr W. Forbes Tel: Braemar (033 83) 676	
15b		Glen Clunie and Devil's Elbow	*INVERCAULD Capt. A.A.C. Farquharson, MC per Factor Invercauld Estates Office Braemar	Derek P. Petrie Factor Tel: Breamar (033 83) 224 or P Fraser Head Stalker Tel: Braemar (033 83) 267	
15d		From Glen Shee	DALMUNZIE	Tel: Glenshee (025 085) 226	
15c			FEALAR Spearman Trustees per Atholl Estates, Estate Office Blair Atholl, Perthshire	The factor Atholl Estates Office Tel: Blair Atholl (079 681) 355	

* East Grampian Deer Management Group Member

15e	Lochnagar Broad Cairn Group	All routes	*BALMORAL The Balmoral Estates' Trustees Balmoral Estate Office Balmoral Ballater Aberdeenshire AB3 5TB	The Factor Estate Office Tel: Crathie (033 84) 334 or Countryside Ranger Tel: Ballater (0338) 55434	Ranger/Naturalist service at Spittal of Glenmuick provides full access information.
15e		From west Glen Callater	*INVERCAULD Capt A.A.C. Farquharson, MC per Factor Invercauld Estates Office Braemar	R.Fyvie Stables Invercauld Tel: Braemar (033 83) 227	
15e		From south Glen Clova Glen Doll	*AIRLIE per Airlie Estates Office Cortachy	A. Mearns Rottal Lodge Cottage Glenclova Tel: Clova (057 55) 230	
15e	Mount Keen	Glen Tanar	*GLEN TANAR Glen Tanar Sporting Co. Estate Office, Aboyne	J. Oswald Tel: Aboyne (0339) 2393	
15e		Glen Muick	*GLENMUICK per Savills 12 Clerk Street Brechin Angus DD9 6AE	P.R. Robertson Head Keeper's House Glenmuick Tel: Ballater (0338) 55403	

* East Grampian Deer Management Group Member

Map/Estate Reference	Mountain or Mountain Group	Approaches	Estate	Contact	Remarks
15e		Glenesk	*DALHOUSIE per Dalhousie Estate Office Brechin	F.Taylor Invermark Tel: Tarfside (035 67) 208	Public car park at Invermark.
15e	Carn t-Sagairt Mor Tolmount	Glen Callater	*INVERCAULD Capt. A.A.C.Farquharson,MC per Factor Invercauld Estates Office Braemar	R. Fyvie Stables Invercauld Tel: Braemar (033 83) 227	
15e		Glen Doll	*AIRLIE per Airlie Estates Office Cortachy	A. Mearns Rottal Lodge Cottage Glenclova Tel: Clova (057 55) 230	
15e	Glas Maol Cairn of Claise	A93	*INVERCAULD (as above)	R. Fyvie (as above)	
15e		Glen Isla Caenlochan	*TULCHAN Rt Hon the Earl of Inchcape per Arthur Young Estate Mangement Manor Street Forfar DD8 1EX	D.Grant Tulchan Lodge Glenisla Tel: Glenisla (057 582) 264	Parking at Linns Bridge only.

* East Grampian Deer Management Group Member

15e	Driesh Mayar	Glen Prosen	*GLENPROSEN Executors of the late Arthur Strutt per West Highland Estates 7 Argyll Street Oban	A,. Boath Craig Lodge Cottage Glenprosen,Kirriemuir Tel: Cortachy (057 54) 314
15e		Glen Doll	*AIRLIE (as above)	A. Mearns (as above)
15e		Glen Isla	*TULCHAN (as above)	D. Grant (as above)
15e	Ben Tirran	Glen Clova	*AIRLIE per Airlie Estates Office Cortachy	A. Mearns Rottal Lodge Cottage Glenclova Tel: Clova (057 55) 230

* East Grampian Deer Management Group Member

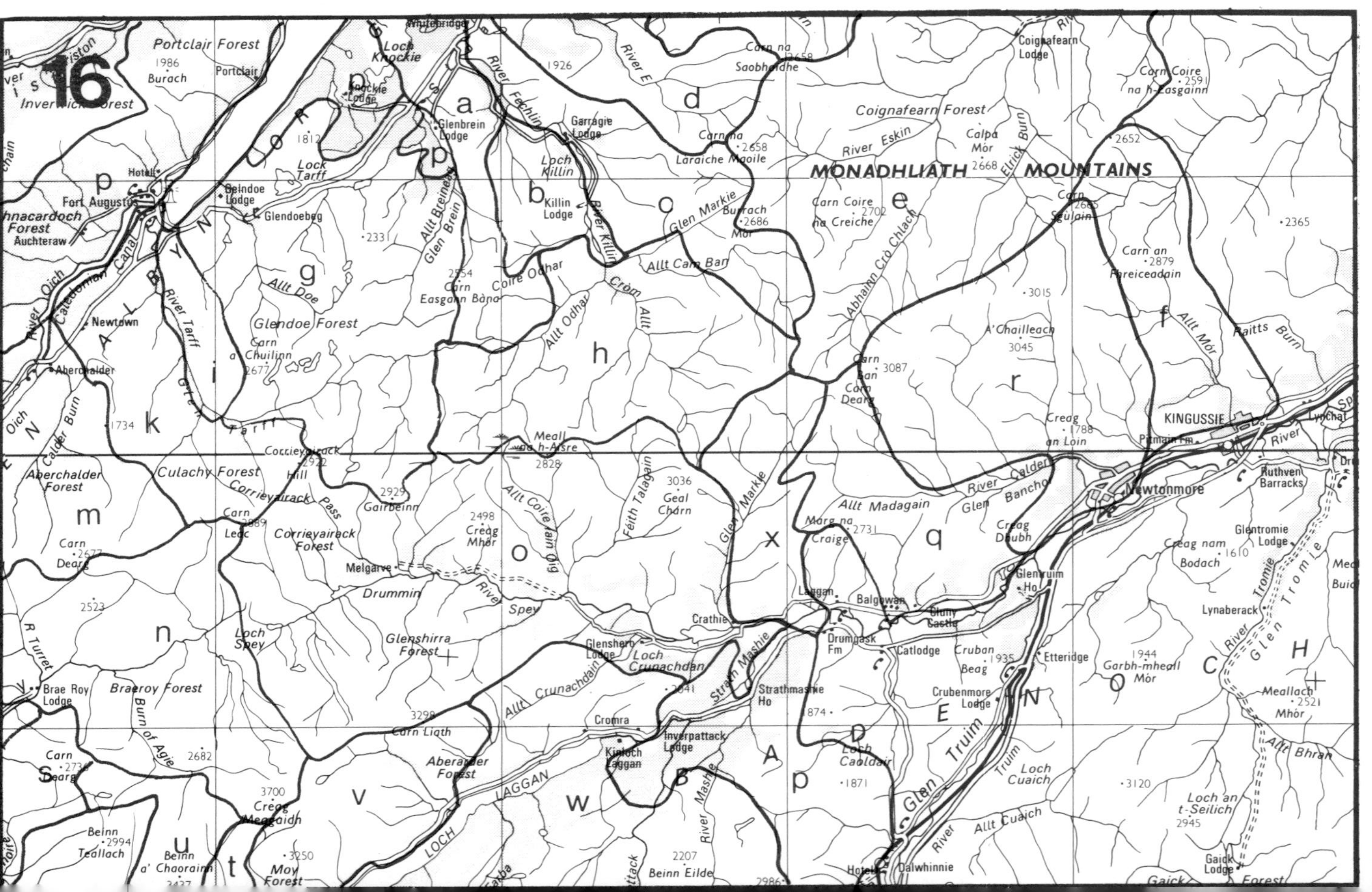
16
MONADHLIATH MOUNTAINS
KINGUSSIE
Newtonmore
Ruthven Barracks
Fort Augustus
Newtown
Aberchalder
Auchteraw
Caledonian Canal
River Oich
Calder Burn
Portclair Forest
Glendoe Forest
Glendoe Lodge
Glendoebeg
Lock Tarff
Loch Knockie
Knockie Lodge
Glenbrein Lodge
Glen Brein
River Fechlin
Loch Killin
Killin Lodge
Garragie Lodge
River Killin
Glen Markie
Coignafearn Forest
Coignafearn Lodge
River Eskin
River Tarff
Corrieyairack Pass
Corrieyairack Forest
Culachy Forest
Aberchalder Forest
Braeroy Forest
Brae Roy Lodge
R Turret
Burn of Agie
Loch Spey
River Spey
Melgarve
Drummin
Glenshirra Forest
Gairbeinn
Meall na h-Aisre
Geal Charn
Crathie
Glenshero Lodge
Loch Crunachdan
Laggan
Drumgask Fm
Balgowan
Catlodge
Cluny Castle
Strathmashie Ho
Strath Mashie
Kinloch Laggan
Inverpattack Lodge
Cromra
Aberarder Forest
Carn Liath
LOCH LAGGAN
Creag Meagaidh
Moy Forest
Beinn a' Chaorainn
Beinn Teallach
Beinn Eilde
River Mashie
Creag Dhubh
Glen Banchor
Glentromie Lodge
Glen Tromie
Lynaberack
Etteridge
Crubenmore Lodge
Glen Truim
Loch Cuaich
Dalwhinnie
Garbh-mheall Mòr
Loch an t-Seilich
Gaick Lodge

Map 16 — Monadh Liath — Creag Meagaidh

Reference	Estate Name
16a	DELL
16b	KILLIN
16c	GARRAGIE
16d	CORRIEGARTH
16e	COIGNAFEARN
16f	PITMAIN
16g	GLENDOE
16h	STRONELAIRG
16i	ARDACHY
16k	GULLACHY (CULACHY)
16m	ABERCHALDER
16n	BRAEROY
16o	GLENSHIRRA & SHERAMORE
16p	FORESTRY COMMISSION
16q	CLUNY
16r	GLEN BANCHOR
16s	GLEN ROY
16t	MOY
16u	TULLOCH
16v	CREAG MEAGAIDH
16w	ARDVERIKIE
16x	MOY LODGE

Hills

Monadh Liath Mountains
Carn a' Chuilinn
Carn Easgann Bana

Creag Meagaidh
Beinn a' Chaorainn
Beinn Teallach

Map/Estate Reference	Mountain or Mountain Group	Approaches	Estate	Contact	Remarks
16r	Monadh Liath Mountains	Glen Banchor	GLEN BANCHOR M.J. Haywood Banchor Mains Newtonmore, Inverness-shire	M.J. Haywood Banchor Mains Tel: Newtonmore (054 03) 215	Parking on Glen road beside 'PRIVATE' sign. No vehicles past this point please.
16q		Strath an Eilich	CLUNY	The Keeper Tel: Laggan (052 84) 229	
16x		Glen Markie	MOY LODGE per Ardverikie Estate Office Kinlochlaggan Newtonmore PH20 1BY	The Keeper Tel: Laggan (052 84) 229	
16f		From Kingussie	PITMAIN Lucas Aardenburg Pitmain Lodge Kingussie	Mr W. Dey Keeper's House Kingussie Tel Kingussie, (054 02) 237	Estate huts at Dulnain & Corrour available for emergency use. No camping please.
16e		From north	COIGNAFEARN		
16d		From north- west	CORRIEGARTH per Savills 12 Clerk Street Brechin, Angus DD9 6AE		

16c			GARRAGIE Charles Connel Garragie Estate by Fort Augustus Inverness-shire	
16a			DELL per Finlayson Hughes 45 Church Street Inverness IV1 1DR	The Keeper Tel: Gorthleck (045 63) 348
16b			KILLIN James Barr Killin Estate Killin, Inverness-shire	Tel: Gorthleck (045 63) 660
16h		From west	STRONELAIRG Charles Connel Garragie Estate by Fort Augustus Inverness-shire	
16g	Carn a' Chuillin Carn Easgann Bana	From Glendoebeg (B862)	GLENDOE Major M.S. Vernon per Farm Manager Borland Farm by Fort Augustus Inverness-shire	

Map/Estate Reference	Mountain or Mountain Group	Approaches	Estate	Contact	Remarks
16a		Glen Brein	DELL (as above)		
16i		Glen Tarff	ARDACHY		
16k			GULLACHY (CULACHY)		
16v	Creag Meagaidh	Coire Ardair Moy Coire	CREAG MEAGAIDH Nature Conservancy Council 17 Rubislaw Terrace Aberdeen AB1 1XE	David Gowans Head Warden Achantoul, Aviemore Tel: Aviemore (0479) 810477	The public are welcome to the National Nature Reserve at all times. Please read the signs and abide by their requests
16o		From north	GLENSHIRRA & SHERAMORE British Alcan Aluminium PLC per West Highland Estates Office 33 High Street Fort William	West Highland Estates Office 33 High Street Fort William Tel: Fort William (0397) 2433	
16n		From west	BRAEROY per Finlayson Hughes 45 Church Street Inverness IV1 1DR		
16u		From south	TULLOCH		

16t			MOY Nature Conservancy Council 17 Rubislaw Terrace Aberdeen AB1 1XE	R.S. Ogilvy Fountain Forestry Inverness Tel: Inverness (0463) 224949
16n	Beinn a' Chaorainn Beinn Teallach	From north	BRAEROY per Finlayson Hughes 45 Church Street Inverness IV1 1DR	
16v		From east and south Loch Moy	CREAG MEAGAIDH Nature Conservancy Council 17 Rubislaw Terrace Aberdeen AB1 1XE	David Gowans Head Warden Achnatoul Aviemore Tel: Aviemore (0479) 810477
16t			MOY Nature Conservancy Council 17 Rubislaw Terrace Aberdeen AB1 1XE	R.S. Ogilvy Fountain Forestry Inverness Tel: Inverness (0463) 224949
16u			TULLOCH	

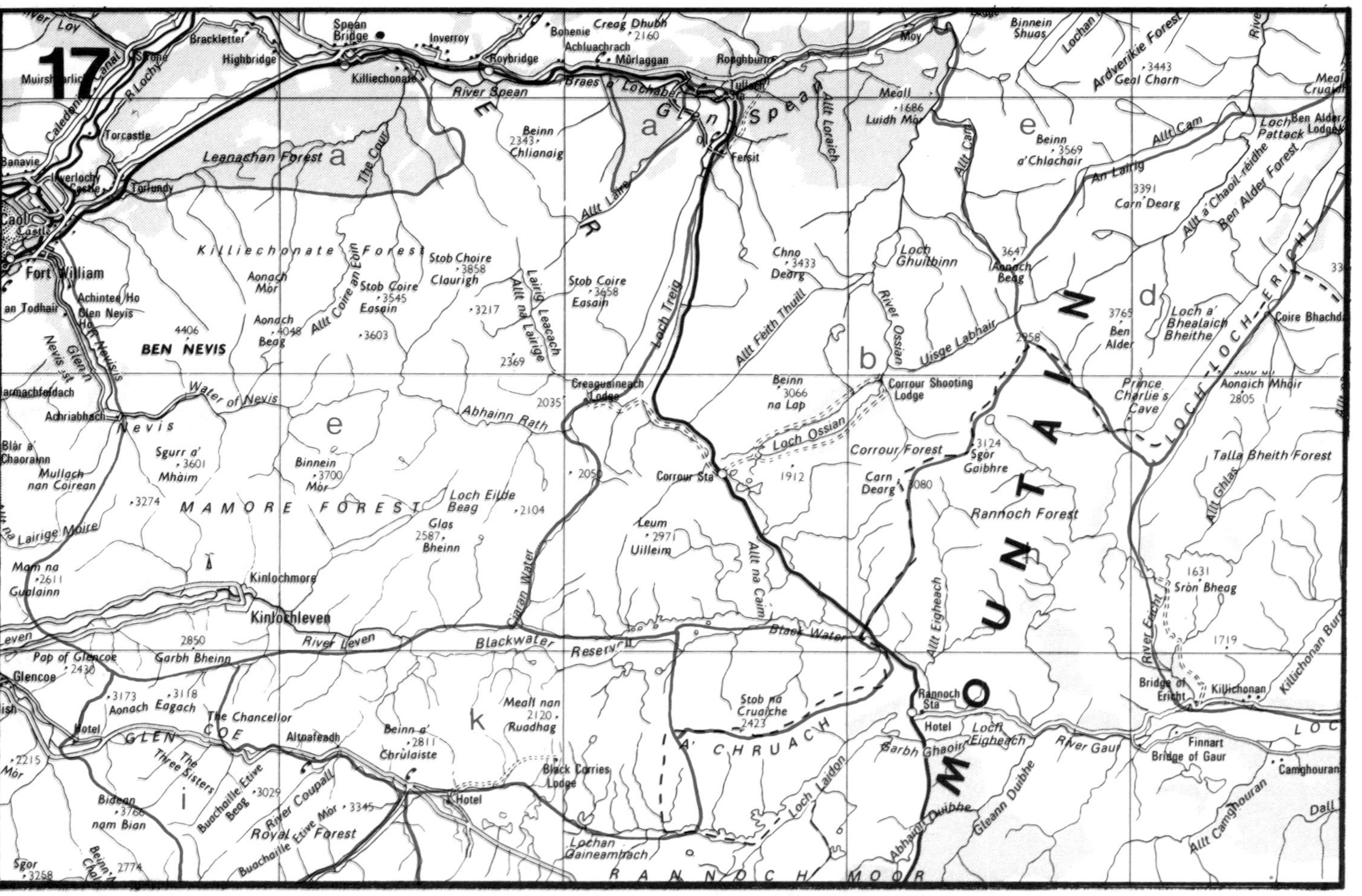

17
Fort William
BEN NEVIS
4406
Glen Nevis
Water of Nevis
Spean Bridge
Roybridge
River Spean
Killiechonate
Killiechonate Forest
Leanachan Forest
Stob Choire Claurigh
Aonach Mòr
Aonach Beag
MAMORE FOREST
Binnein Mòr
Sgurr a' Mhàim
Loch Eilde Beag
Kinlochleven
Kinlochmore
River Leven
Blackwater Reservoir
Aonach Eagach
Pap of Glencoe
Glencoe
GLEN COE
The Three Sisters
Buachaille Etive Beag
Buachaille Etive Mòr
Royal Forest
Loch Treig
Creaguaineach Lodge
Corrour Sta
Loch Ossian
Corrour Shooting Lodge
Corrour Forest
River Ossian
Beinn na Lap
Chno Dearg
Rannoch Sta
Loch Eigheach
Rannoch Forest
RANNOCH MOOR
LOCH ERICHT
Ben Alder
Prince Charlie's Cave
Ben Alder Forest
Loch Laidon
River Gaur
Bridge of Gaur
Talla Bheith Forest
MOUNTAIN

Map 17 — Ben Nevis — Ben Alder

Reference	Estate Name
17a	FORESTRY COMMISSION
17b	CORROUR
17c	ARDVERIKIE
17d	BEN ALDER
17e	KILLIECHONATE & MAMORES
17g	DUNAN
17h	CAMUSERICHT
17i	GLEN COE & DALNESS
17k	BLACK CORRIES

Hills

Beinn a' Chlachair
Creag Pitridh
Beinnein Shuas
Geal Charn
Stob Coire Easain
Stob a' Choire Mheadhoin
Grey Corries
Aonachs
Ben Nevis
The Mamores
Carn Dearg
Sgor Gaibhre
Beinn na Lap
Chno Dearg
Stob Coire Sgriodain
Ben Alder
Aonach Beag Group
Aonach Eagach
Meall nan Ruadhag
Stob na Cruaiche
Beinn a' Chrulaiste
Devil's Staircase

Map/Estate Reference	Mountain or Mountain Group	Approaches	Estate	Contact	Remarks
17c	Beinn a' Chlachair Creag Pitridh Geal Charn Bheinn Shuas	Loch Laggan and River Pattack	ARDVERIKIE Ardverikie Estate Ltd Kinlochlaggan Newtonmore PH20 1BY	G.A.D. Chalmer Factor, Estate Office Kinlochlaggan Tel: Laggan (052 84) 300	
17d		From south	BEN ALDER P.H. Byam-Cook Ben Alder Estate Dalwhinnie Inverness-shire	George Oswald Head Stalker Ben Alder Cottages Dalwhinnie Tel: Dalwhinnie (052 82) 244 or 230	Keys can be had from G. Oswald to get cars to Loch Pattack iron shed by arrangement but estate will not be liable for damage to cars by estate ponies which sometimes eat cars!
17e	Stob Coire Easain Stob a' Choire Mheadhoin Grey Corries Aonachs Ben Nevis The Mamores	All routes	KILLIECHONATE & MAMORE British Alcan Aluminium PLC per West Highland Estates Office 33 High Street Fort William	West Highland Estates Office 33 High Street Fort William Tel: Fort William (0397) 2433	
17a		Torlundy Spean Bridge	FORESTRY COMMISSION 21 Church Street Inverness IV1 1EL	Lochaber Forest District Torlundy, Fort William Tel: Fort William (0397) 2184	

17g	Carn Dearg Sgor Gaibhre	Rannoch Station	DUNAN Hamish McCorquodale Dunan Lodge Rannoch Station	Colin Robertson Camusericht Farm Rannoch Station Tel: Bridge of Gaur (088 23) 230	
17h			CAMUSERICHT Mr & Mrs David Irvine Camusericht Lodge Bridge of Gaur Rannoch Station	West Highland Estates Office 7 Argyll Stree, Oban Tel: Oban (0631) 63617	
17b	Beinn na Lap Chno Dearg Stob Coire Sgriodain	All routes	CORROUR Pollock & Corrour Ltd Corrour Estate Corrour Fort William	Ted Piggott Head Stalker Corrour Estate or Warden at Youth Hostel Corrour Station	No vehicles allowed on Estate. Parking on A86 or by Fersit. Please keep to paths and avoid estate during stalking.
17c	Ben Alder Aonach Beag Group	From north	ARDVERIKIE Ardverikie Estate Ltd Kinlochlaggan Newtonmore PH20 1BY	G.A.D. Chalmer Factor Estate Office, Kinlochlaggan Tel: Laggan (052 84) 300	

Map/Estate Reference	Mountain or Mountain Group	Approaches	Estate	Contact	Remarks
17d		All routes	BEN ALDER P.H. Byam-Cook Ben Alder Estate Dalwhinnie	George Oswald Head Stalker Ben Alder Cottages Dalwhinnie Tel: Dalwhinnie (052 82) 244 or 230	Keys can be had from G. Oswald to get cars to Loch Pattack iron shed by arrangement but estate will not be liable for damage to cars by estate ponies which sometimes eat cars!
17h		Loch Rannoch Benalder Cottage	CAMUSERICHT (as above)	Ted Piggott (as above)	
17b		Loch Ossian	CORROUR	Ted Piggot (as above)	
17i	Aonach Eagach Meall nan Ruadhag Stob na Cruaiche Beinn a' Chrulaiste Devil's Staircase	All routes	GLENCOE & DALNESS National Trust for Scotland 5 Charlotte Square Edinburgh EH2 4DU	The Ranger Achnambeithach Glencoe Tel: Ballachulish (085 52) 311 or 307	
17k			BLACK CORRIES Vicomte Adolphe de Speolbergh Black Corries Estate Glencoe	Peter O'Connell Black Corries Estate Tel: Kingshouse (085 56) 272	No camping in immediate vicinity of Kingshouse and Lodge. Cars will only be allowed to park on road between Kingshouse and Lodge **with permission**

17e	From north	KILLIECHONATE & MAMORE British Alcan Aluminium PLC per West Highland Estates Office 33 High Street Fort William	West Highland Estate Office 33 High Street, Fort William Tel: Fort William (0397) 2433	
17b		CORROUR Pollock & Corrour Ltd Corrour Estate Corrour Fort William	Ted Piggott Head Stalker Corrour Estate or Warden at Youth Hostel Corrour Station	No vehicles allowed on Estate. Parking on A86 or by Fersit. Please keep to paths and avoid Estate during stalking.

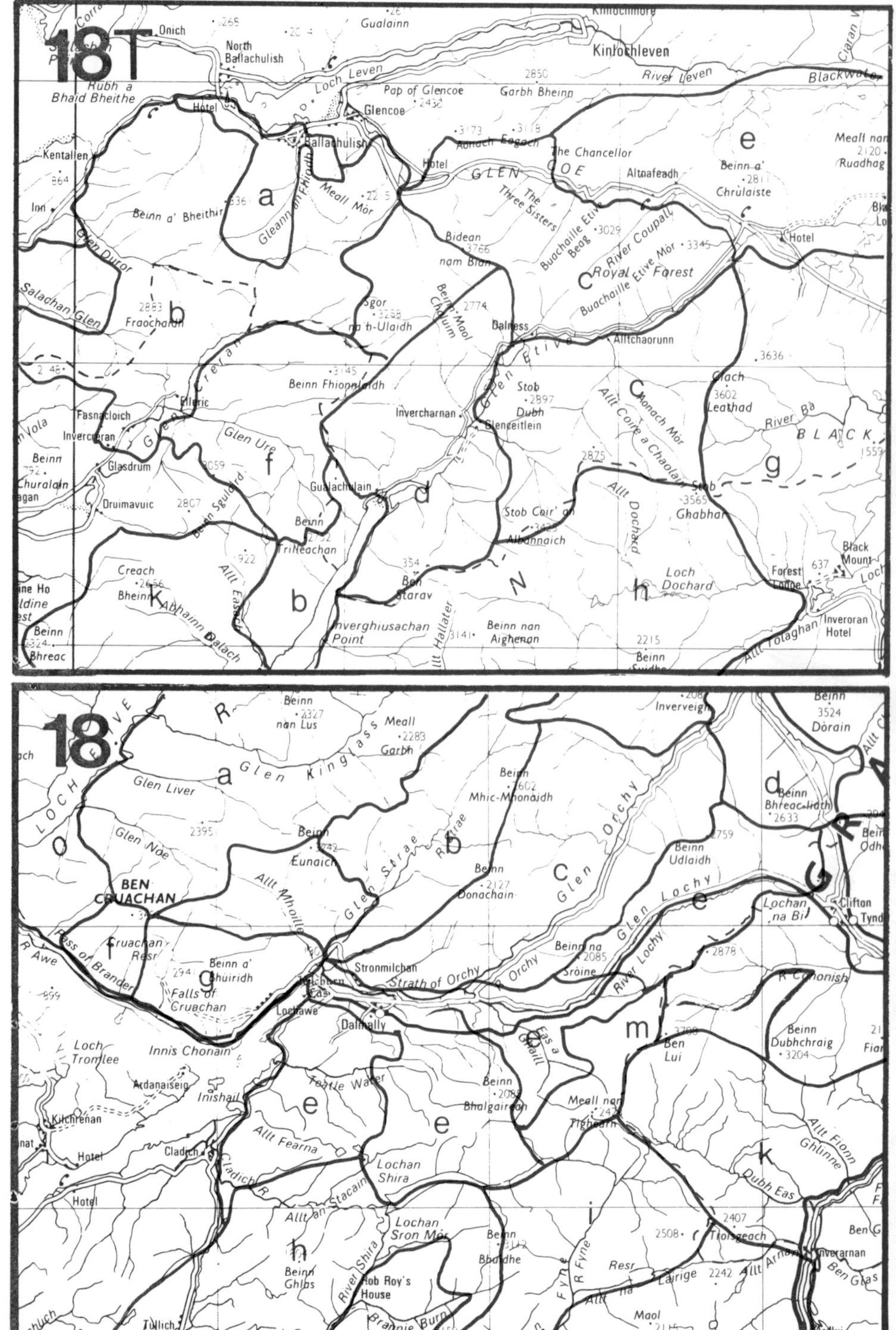

18T
18

Map 18T — Glen Coe — Blackmount

Reference	Estate Name
18T/a	BALLACHULISH
18T/b	FORESTRY COMMISSION
18T/c	GLENCOE & DALNESS
18T/d	GLEN ETIVE
18T/e	BLACK CORRIES
18T/f	GLENCRERAN
18T/g	BLACKMOUNT
18T/h	GLENKINGLAS
18T/k	ARDCHATTAN

Hills

Bidean nam Bian Group
Buachaille Etive Mor
Buachaille Etive Beag
Beinn a' Bheithir
Sgor na h-Ulaidh
Creise
Meall a' Bhuiridh
Stob Ghabhar
Clach Leathad
Beinn Fhionnlaidh
Beinn Sgulaird
Beinn Trilleachan
Creach Bheinn Group
Ben Starav
Beinn a' Chrulaiste
Devil's Staircase

Map 18B — Ben Cruachan — Ben Lui

References	Estate Name
18B/a	GLENKINGLASS
18B/b	DUILETTER
18B/c	CRAIG
18B/d	AUCH
18B/e	FORESTRY COMMISSION
18B/f	INVERAWE
18B/g	CASTLES FARM
18B/h	ARGYLL
18B/i	ARDKINGLASS
18B/k	GLENFALLOCH
18B/m	BEN LUI NATIONAL NATURE RESERVE

Hills

Ben Cruachan
Beinn Eunaich
Beinn Mhic-Mhonaidh
Beinn Donachain
Beinn Udlaidh
Beinn Bhreac-liath
Beinn Lui Group
Beinn Bhuidhe

Map/Estate Reference	Mountain or Mountain Group	Approaches	Estate	Contact	Remarks
18T/a	Beinn a'Bheithir	Ballachulish Village	BALLACHULISH per Major J V Parnell Dal Bhan, Onich Fort William PH33 6RY	Ronald McLaughlan Gorteneorn Farm Ballachulish Tel: Ballachulish (085 52) 263	
18T/b		All routes	FORESTRY COMMISSION Portcullis House 21 India Street Glasgow G2 4PL	Lorne Forest District Millpark Road,Oban Argyll Tel: Oban (0631) 66155	
18T/c	Bidean nam Bian Group Buachaille Etive Beag Buachaille Etive Mor	All routes	GLENCOE & DALNESS National Trust for Scotland 5 Charlotte Square Edinburgh	The Ranger Achnambeithach Glencoe Tel: Ballachulish (085 52) 311 or 307	
18T/d		Glen Etive	GLEN ETIVE Mr Robin Fleming Black Mount Bridge of Orchy Argyll	Jock Fraser Glen Etive Tel: Kingshouse (085 56) 277 or Colin Fraser Tel: Tyndrum (083 84) 283	

18T/e	Beinn a'Chrulaiste Devil's Staircase	From A82 and Kingshouse	BLACK CORRIES Vicomte Adolphe de Speolbergh Black Corries Estate Glencoe	Peter O'Connell Black Corries Estate Tel: Kingshouse (085 56) 272	No camping in immediate vicinity of Kingshouse and Lodge. Cars will only be allowed to park on road between Kingshouse and Lodge **with permission.**
18T/f	Sgor na h-Ulaidh	Glen Creran	GLENCRERAN P. Zvegintz per West Higjland Estates Office, Argyll Street Oban PA34 5SG	C. Livingston Stalker's Cottage Glenreran Appin Argyll	
18T/b			FORESTRY COMMISSION Portcullis House 21 India Street Glasgow G2 4PL	Lorne Forest District Millpark Road, Oban Argyll Tel: Oban (0631) 66155	
18T/d		Glen Etive	GLEN ETIVE Mr Robin Fleming Black Mount Bridge of Orchy Argyll	Jock Fraser Glen Etive Tel: Kingshouse (085 56) 277 or Colin Fraser Tel: Tyndrum (083 84) 283	

Map/Estate Reference	Mountain or Mountain Group	Approaches	Estate	Contact	Remarks
18T/g	Creise Meall a'Bhuiridh Stob Ghabhar Clach Leathad	From A82 and Victoria Bridge	BLACKMOUNT Mr Robin Fleming Black Mount Bridge of Orchy Argyll	Hamish Menzies Tel: Tyndrum (083 84) 225 or Ian MacRae Tel: Tyndrum (083 84) 269	Parking at Victoria Bridge and Achallader Farmhouse
18T/c			GLENCOE & DALNESS National Trust for Scotland 5 Charlotte Square Edinburgh	The Ranger Achnambeithach Glencoe Tel: Ballachulish (085 52) 311 or 307	
18T/d		From west	GLEN ETIVE (as above)	Jock Fraser (as above)	
18T/h		From south	GLENKINGLASS The Hon. Mrs J B Schuster & The Hon. Mrs R E Fleming per West Highland Estates Office 7 Argyll Street Oban PA34 5SG (0631) 63617	Tim Healy Stalker Ardmaddy Taynuilt Argyll Tel: Taynuilt (086 62) 271	No camping - No vehicular access

18T/d	Beinn Fhionnlaidh Beinn Sgulaird Beinn Trilleachan	From north	GLEN ETIVE Mr Robin Fleming Black Mount Bridge of Orchy Argyll	Jock Fraser Glen Etive Tel: Kingshouse (085 56) 277 or Colin Fraser Tel: Tyndrum (083 84) 283
18T/f		From west	GLENCRERAN P. Zvegintz per West Highland Estates Office Argyll Street Oban PA34 5SG	C. Livingston Stalker's Cottage Glencreran Appin Argyll
18T/k		From south	ARDCHATTAN Mrs James Troughton Ardchattan Priory Connel Argyll	Malcolm MacDonald Ardachy Farm Ardchattan Tel: Connel (063 171) 274
18T/k	Creach Bheinn Group	All routes	ARDCHATTAN (as above)	Malcolm MacDonald (as above)
18T/b		From west	FORESTRY COMMISSION Portcullis House 21 India Street Glasgow G2 4PL	Lorne Forest District Millpark Road, Oban Argyll Tel: Oban (0631)66155

Map/Estate Reference	Mountain or Mountain Group	Approaches	Estate	Contact	Remarks
18T/h	Ben Starav	All routes	GLENKINGLASS (as above)	Tim Healy (as above)	
18T/d		From north	GLEN ETIVE Mr Robin Fleming Black Mount Bridge of Orchy Argyll	Jock Fraser Glen Etive Tel: Kingshouse (085 56) 277 or Colin Fraser Tel: Tyndrum (083 84) 283	
18B/g	Ben Cruachan	Loch Aweside	CASTLES FARM De Windstreken & Co. Lochawe, Dalmally Argyll	A. Gray at Castles Farm Tel: Dalmally (083 82) 247	
18B/a		From north	GLENKINGLASS The Hon. Mrs J.B. Schuster The Hon. Mrs R.E. Fleming per West Highland Estates Office 7 Argyll Street Oban PA34 5SG (0631) 63617	Tim Healy Stalker Ardmaddy Taynuilt Tel: Taynuilt (086 62) 271	No camping - No vehicular access
18B/f		From west	INVERAWE		

18B/b		From east	DUILETTER per West Highland Estates Office 7 Argyll Street Oban PA34 5SG	THE KEEPER Alistair MacLeod Tel: Dalmally (083 82) 217
18B/c	Beinn Mhic-Mhonaidh Beinn Donachain	All routes	CRAIG Mr McLaren Craig Farm, Dalmally Argyll	Tel: Dalmally (083 82) 213
18B/b		Glen Strae	DUILETTER (as above)	The keeper (as above)
18B/d	Beinn Udlaidh Beinn Bhreac-liath	From north-east	AUCH Lord Trevor Auch Estate, Bridge of Orchy Argyll	C. Macdonald Auch Tel: Tyndrum (083 84) 233
18B/e		Glen Lochy	FORESTRY COMMISSION Portcullis House 21 India Street Glasgow G2 4PL	Loch Awe Forest District Whitegates, Lochgilphead Argyll Tel: Lochgilphead (0546) 2518
18B/e	Ben Lui Group	Glen Lochy	FORESTRY COMMISSION (as above)	

Map/Estate Reference	Mountain or Mountain Group	Approaches	Estate	Contact	Remarks
18B/k		Glen Falloch	GLENFALLOCH E.J. & R.N. Lowes Glenfalloch Lodge Ardlui	D. Neilson Clisham Cottage, Glenfalloch Tel: Inveruglas (030 14) 229	
18B/m	Ben Lui Group		BEN LUI NATIONAL NATURE RESERVE The Castle Loch Lomond Park Balloch	Reserve Warden Andrew Campbell Glensalloch Road, Barcaldine Oban Tel: (063 172) 363	
18B/i	Beinn Bhuidhe	Glen Fyne	ARDKINGLAS Mr John Noble Ardkinglas House Cairndow, Argyll	Tel: Cairndow (049 96) 217	
18B/h		From south-west Glen Shira	ARGYLL Trustees of the Tenth Duke of Argyll Argyll Estates Office, Cherry Park Inveraray	P.M. Fairweather Argyll Estates Office Inveraray Tel: Inveraray (0499) 2203	Park at locked gate in Glen Shira.
18B/e		From north	FORESTRY COMMISSION (as above)		

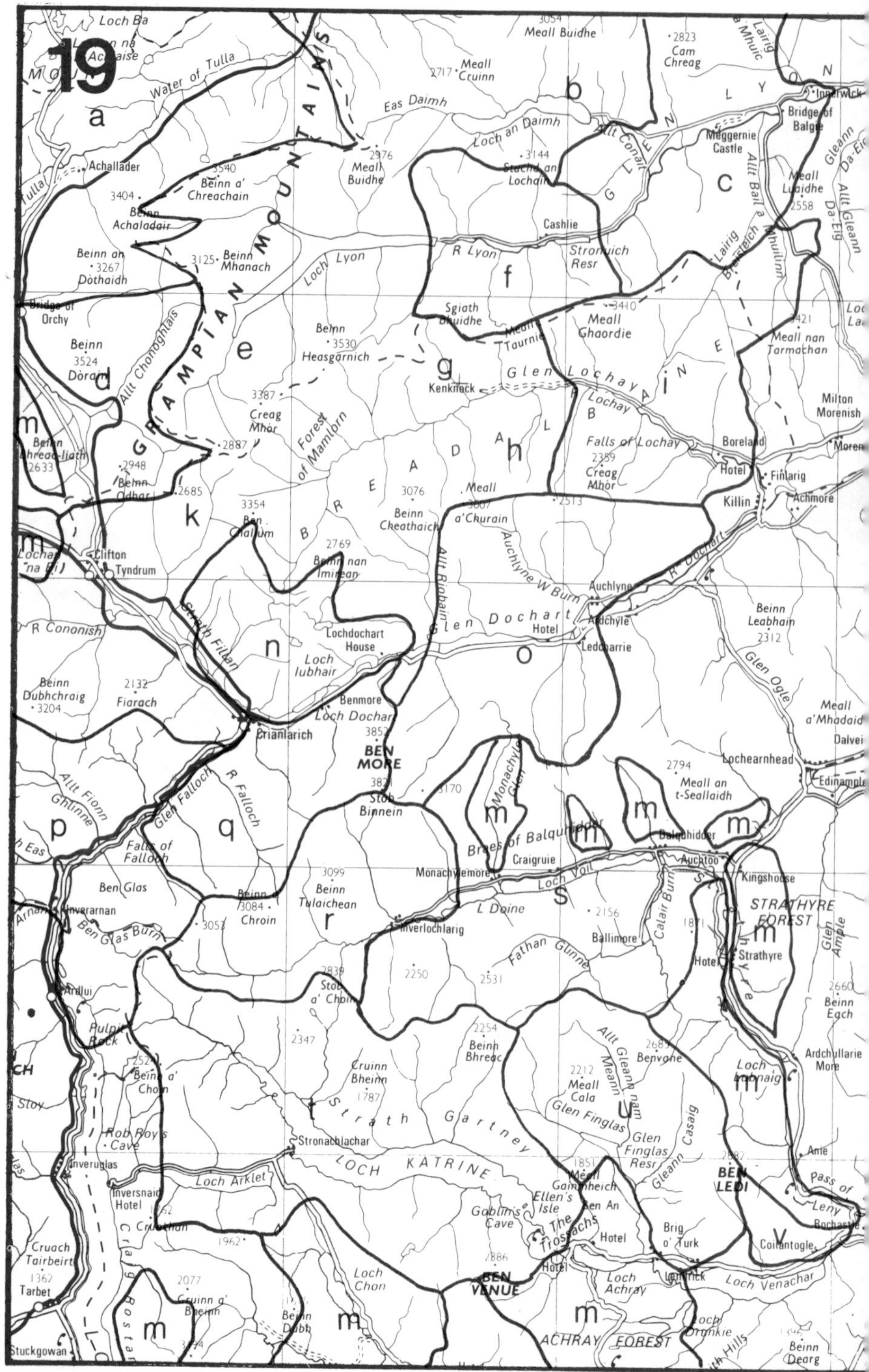
19
Loch Ba
Water of Tulla
a
b
c
Meall Buidhe
3054
2823
Cam Chreag
2717
Meall Cruinn
Eas Daimh
Loch an Daimh
GLEN LYON
Innerwick
Bridge of Balgie
Meggernie Castle
Achallader
3540
Beinn a' Chreachain
3404
Beinn Achaladair
2976
Meall Buidhe
3144
Stuchd an Lochain
Meall Luaidhe
2558
Cashlie
GRAMPIAN MOUNTAINS
Beinn an Dòthaidh
3267
3125
Beinn Mhanach
Loch Lyon
R Lyon
Stronuich Resr
f
Bridge of Orchy
Beinn Dòrain
3524
Sgiath Bhuidhe
Meall Taurnie
3410
Meall Ghaordie
3421
Meall nan Tarmachan
Allt Chonoghlais
Beinn Heasgarnich
3530
e
g
Kenknock
Glen Lochay
R Lochay
d
3387
Creag Mhor
Forest of Mamlorn
Falls of Lochay
Boreland
Milton Morenish
m
2887
Beinn Chreag-liath
2633
2948
Beinn Odhar
2685
BREADALBANE
h
2359
Creag Mhor
Hotel
Finlarig
Killin
Achmore
3354
Ben Challum
3076
Beinn Cheathaich
Meall a' Churain
3007
2513
k
Clifton
Tyndrum
Loch na Bi
2769
Beinn nan Imirean
Auchlyne W Burn
R Dochart
Auchlyne
Ardchyle
Strath Fillan
R Cononish
Allt Riobain
Glen Dochart
Hotel
Lochdochart House
n
Loch Iubhair
Leddharrie
o
Beinn Leabhain
2312
Glen Ogle
Beinn Dubhchraig
3204
2132
Fiarach
Benmore
Loch Dochart
Crianlarich
3852
BEN MORE
Meall a' Mhadaidh
Dalveich
Monachyle Glen
2794
Meall an t-Seallaidh
Lochearnhead
Edinample
Allt Fionn Ghlinne
Glen Falloch
R Falloch
3821
Stob Binnein
3170
p
q
Braes of Balquhidder
Balquhidder
Auchtoo
Falls of Falloch
Craigruie
Monachylemore
Loch Voil
Kingshouse
Ben Glas
3099
Beinn Tulaichean
Beinn a' Chroin
3084
s
STRATHYRE FOREST
Inverarnan
Ben Glas Burn
3053
r
L Doine
2156
Inverlochlarig
Ballimore
Calair Burn
1871
Fathan Glinne
Strathyre
Hotel
Glen Ample
Ardlui
2839
Stob a' Choin
2250
2531
2660
Beinn Each
Pulpit Rock
2254
Beinn Bhreac
2347
Allt Gleann nam Meann
2685
Benvane
Ardchullarie More
2524
Beinn a' Choin
Cruinn Bheinn
1787
2212
Meall Cala
Loch Lubnaig
Glen Finglas
Strath Gartney
t
u
Rob Roy's Cave
Stronachlachar
Glen Finglas Resr
Gleann Casaig
Anie
LOCH KATRINE
Inveruglas
Loch Arklet
1851
Meall Gainmheich
2882
BEN LEDI
Pass of Leny
Inversnaid Hotel
Cruachan
Ellen's Isle
Goblin's Cave
Ben An
The Trossachs
Hotel
Bochastle
v
Cruach Tairbeirt
1362
1962
Brig o' Turk
Coilantogle
Tarbet
2077
Cruinn a' Bheinn
2386
BEN VENUE
Hotel
Loch Chon
Loch Achray
Lendrick
Loch Venachar
Beinn Dubh
Loch Drunkie
Stuckgowan
ACHRAY FOREST
Beinn Dearg

Map 19 — Bridge of Orchy — Crianlarich — Trossachs

Reference	Estate Name
19a	BLACKMOUNT
19b	LOCHS
19c	MEGGERNIE
19d	AUCH
19e	BEN CHALLUM
19f	CASHLIE
19g	GLEN LOCHAY
19h	INVERMEARAN
19i	BORELAND
19k	AUCHESSAN
19m	FORESTRY COMMISSION
19n	LOCHDOCHART
19o	AUCHLYNE & SUIE
19p	GLENFALLOCH
19q	BENMORE FARM
19r	INVERLOCHLARIG
19s	BALQUHIDDER
19t	LOCH KATRINE
19u	GLENFINLAS
19v	MILTON OF CALLANDER

Hills

Meall Buidhe
Beinn Achaladair Group
Beinn Dorain
Stuchd an Lochain
Meall Ghaordie
Meall nan Tarmachan
Meall Glas
Ben Challum
Creag Mhor

Beinn Heasgarnich
Glen Lochay
Cruach Ardrain
An Caisteal Group
Beinn a' Chroin
Beinn Tulaichean
Ben More
Stob Binnein
Ben Venue
Ben A'n
Ben Ledi

Map/Estate Reference	Mountain or Mountain Group	Approaches	Estate	Contact	Remarks
19m	Meall Buidhe	Loch Rannoch	FORESTRY COMMISSION Portcullis House 21 India Street Glasgow G2 4PL	Aberfoyle Forest District Ballanton Office, Aberfoyle Tel: Aberfoyle (087 72) 383	
19c		From east	MEGGERNIE Mrs Searle Meggernie Estate Bridge of Balgie Aberfeldy	C. Grant Keeper's Cottage Bridge of Balgie, Aberfeldy Tel: Bridge of Balgie (088 76) 247	
19f		From south Glen Lyon	CASHLIE W. Porter Cashlie Estate Bridge of Balgie Aberfeldy	D. Sinclair Keeper Cashlie Estate, Bridge of Balgie Aberfeldy Tel: Bridge of Balgie (088 76) 237	
19a	Beinn Achaladair Group Beinn Dorain	Achallader	BLACKMOUNT Mr Robin Fleming Black Mount Bridge of Orchy Argyll	Hamish Menzies Tel: Tyndrum (083 84) 225 or Ian Macrae Tel: Tyndrum (083 84) 269	Parking at Victoria Bridge and Achalladar Farmhouse.

19d		Auch Gleann	AUCH Lord Trevor Auch Estate, Bridge of Orchy Argyll	C. Macdonald Auch Tel: Tyndrum (083 84) 233	
19b	Meall Buidhe Stuchd an Lochain	Loch an Daimh	LOCHS Lady Julia Wills Lochs Estate Glenlyon Aberfeldy	W. Mason Croc-na-Keys Lochs Estate, Glenlyon Aberfeldy Tel: Bridge of Balgie (088 76) 224	
19f		Cashlie	CASHLIE W. Porter Cashlie Estate Bridge of Balgie Aberfeldy	D. Sinclair Keeper Cashlie Estate Bridge of Balgie Aberfeldy Tel: Bridge of Balgie (088 76) 237	
19a		From west	BLACKMOUNT Mr Robin Fleming Black Mount Bridge of Orchy Argyll	Hamish Menzies Tel: Tyndrum (083 84) 225 or Ian MacRae Tel: Tyndrum (083 84) 269	Parking at Victoria Bridge and Achallader Farmhouse.

Map/Estate Reference	Mountain or Mountain Group	Approaches	Estate	Contact	Remarks
19i	Meall Ghaordie	Glen Lochay	BORELAND Judge Stroyan Boreland Killin Perthshire	T. Frost Kennels Cottage Boreland Estate Killin Tel: Killin (056 72) 562	
19f		Glen Lyon	CASHLIE W. Porter Cashlie Estate Bridge of Balgie Aberfeldy	D. Sinclair Keeper Cashlie Estate, Bridge of Balgie Aberfeldy Tel: Bridge of Balgie (088 76) 237	
19i	Meall nan Tarmachan	Loch na Lairige and Killin	BORELAND (as above)	T. frost (as above)	
19c		From north	MEGGERNIE Mrs Searle Meggernie Estate Bridge of Balgie Aberfeldy	C. Grant Keeper's Cottage Bridge of Balgie Aberfeldy Tel: Bridge of Balgie (088 76) 247	

19e	Meall Glas Ben Challum Creag Mhor Beinn Heasgarnich Glen Lochay	Glen Lochay	BEN CHALLUM per Ian M.M. Stewart Lochay Crieff Perthshire	Farm Manager Kenknock Glen Lochay, Killin Perthshire Tel: Killin (056 72) 278
19h			INVERMEARAN	R. Bisset Head Stalker Pubil, Bridge of Balgie Aberfeldy Tel: Bridge of Balgie (088 76) 244
19k		Auchessan Glen Dochart	AUCHESSAN R.N. Mayo Auchessan Estate Crianlarich	D. Cannon Shepherd's House, Auchessan Tel: Crianlarich (083 83) 518
19d		From west	AUCH Lord Trevor Auch Estate, Bridge of Orchy Argyll	C. Macdonald Auch Tel: Tyndrum (083 84) 233
19n		From south	LOCHDOCHART W.J. Christie of Lochdochart Lochdochart Crianlarich	Lachie MacFadyan or Derek Christie Tel: Crianlarich (083 83) 275 or 295

Map/Estate Reference	Mountain or Mountain Group	Approaches	Estate	Contact	Remarks
19p	Cruach Ardrain An Caisteal Group Beinn a' Chroin Beinn Tulaichean	Glen Falloch	GLENFALLOCH E.J. & R.N. Lowes Glenfalloch Lodge Ardlui	D. Neilson Clisham Cottage Glenfalloch Tel: Inveruglas (030 14) 229	
19q		Crainlarich	BENMORE FARM Fulton C. Ronald Keilator Farm Crianlarich Perthshire	Fulton C. Ronald Tel: Crianlarich (083 83) 281	
19m			FORESTRY COMMISSION Portcullis House 21 India Street Glasgow G2 4PL	Aberfoyle Forest District Ballanton Office Aberfoyle Tel: Aberfoyle (087 72) 383	
19r		Inverlochlarig	INVERLOCHLARIG Breas Farming Co. Inverlochlarig, Balquihidder Lochearnhead	J. or M. McNaughton Inverlochlarig Tel: Strathyre (087 74) 232 or 249	Parking/picnic area provided by Braes Farming Co. No dogs during lambing time please.

19o	Ben More Stob Binnein	Glen Dochart	AUCHLYNE & SUIE Mrs E. Paterson & Mrs J. Bowser Auchlyne Killin	G. Coyne Auchlyne, Killin Tel: Killin (056 72) 487	Parking in lay-by on A85. Please keep dogs on leads at all times.
19m		Crianlarich	FORESTRY COMMISSION (as above)		
19q			BENMORE FARM (as above)	Fulton C. Ronald (as above)	
19r		Inverlochlarig	INVERLOCHLARIG (as above)	J. or M. McNaughton (as above)	
19u	Ben Venue Ben A'n	Glen Finglas	GLENFINGLAS John B. Cameron Balbuthie Farm, By Leven Fife	Ian Macfarlane Head Shepherd Tel: Trossachs (087 76) 256	No camping - water catchment area.
19t		All routes	LOCH KATRINE Strathclyde Regional Council Water Department 419 Balmore Road Glasgow G66 2NU	A. Campbell Stronachlacher Tel: Inversnaid (087 786) 210	Parking outwith the catchment area. No camping or pollution of catchment area.

Map/Estate Reference	Mountain or Mountain Group	Approaches	Estate	Contact	Remarks
19m		From south	FORESTRY COMMISSION Portcullis House 21 India Street Glasgow G2 4PL	Aberfoyle Forest District Ballanton Office Aberfoyle Tel: Aberfoyle (087 72) 383	
19u	Ben Ledi	Coilantogle Farm Loch Venachar	MILTON OF CALLANDER Moray Estates Development Co. Estates Office Forres Moray IV36 0ET	W. Scott Milton of Callander Farm Callander Tel: Callander (0877) 30162	Parking very limited on sides of A821. Please do not block farm entrances.
19m		Loch Lubnaig	FORESTRY COMMISSION (as above)	(as above)	
19u		Glen Finglas	GLENFINGLAS (as above)	Ian Macfarlane (as above)	

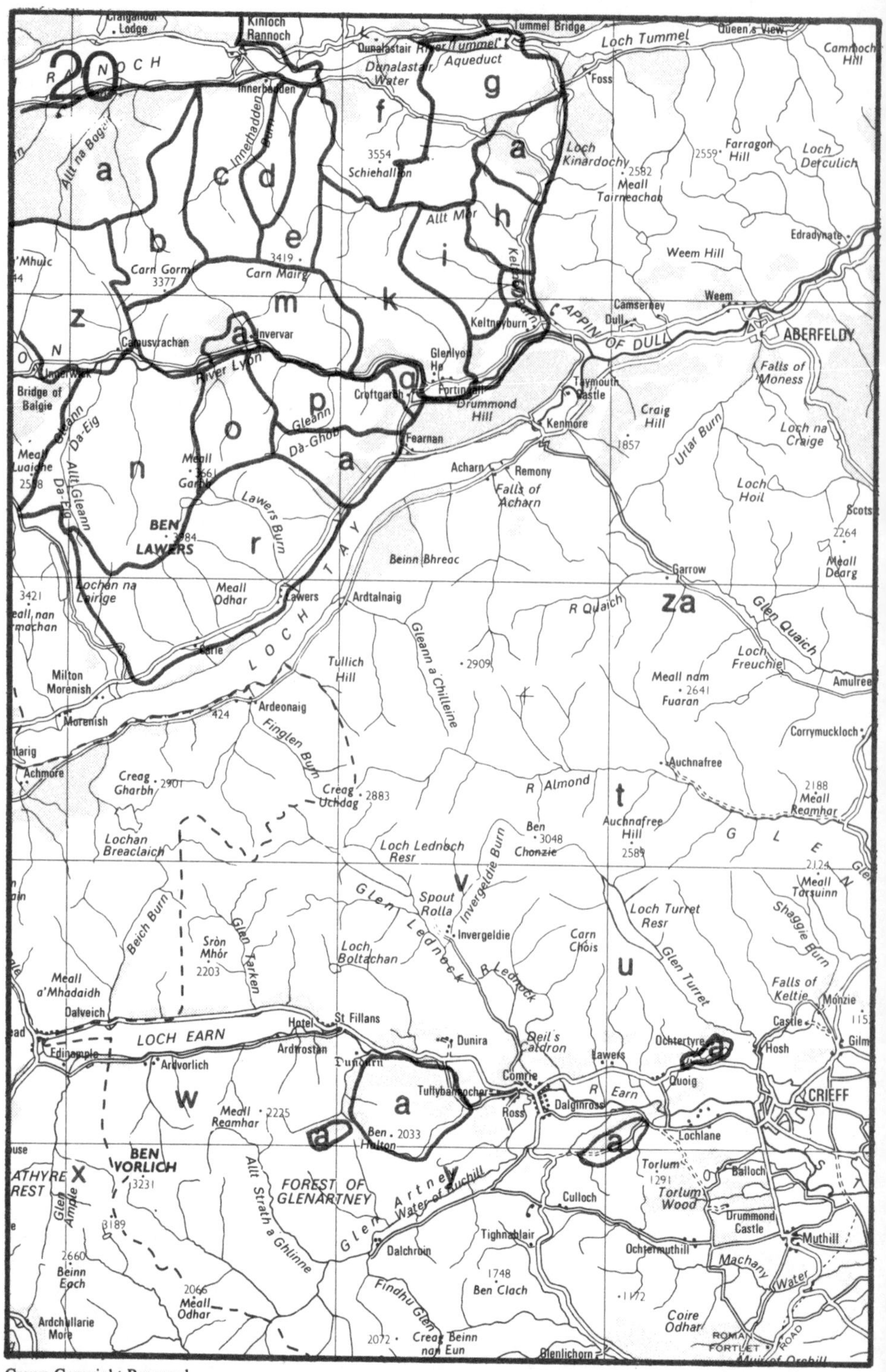

20
Craiganour Lodge
Kinloch Rannoch
Tummel Bridge
Loch Tummel
Queen's View
Cammoch Hill
Dunalastair
River Tummel
Dunalastair Water
Aqueduct
Foss
Innerhadden
Innerhadden Burn
Allt na Bogair
3554
Schiehallion
Loch Kinardochy
2582
Meall Tairneachan
2559
Farragon Hill
Loch Derculich
Allt Mor
Edradynate
Weem Hill
3419
Carn Mairg
Carn Gorm
3377
Keltneyburn
Camserney
Dull
Weem
APPIN OF DULL
ABERFELDY
Camusvrachan
Invervar
River Lyon
Innerwick
Bridge of Balgie
Glenlyon Ho
Fortingall
Croftgarbh
Drummond Hill
Taymouth Castle
Kenmore
Falls of Moness
Craig Hill
Urlar Burn
Loch na Craige
1857
Fearnan
Gleann Da-Ghob
Gleann Da-Eig
Allt Gleann Da-Eig
Meall Luaighe
2558
Meall Garbh
3661
Acharn
Remony
Falls of Acharn
Loch Hoil
Lawers Burn
BEN LAWERS
3984
Beinn Bhreac
2264
Meall Dearg
Garrow
LOCH TAY
3421
Lochan na Lairige
Meall Odhar
Lawers
Ardtalnaig
R Quaich
Glen Quaich
Loch Freuchie
Tullich Hill
Gleann a Chilleine
2909
Meall nam Fuaran
2641
Amulree
Milton Morenish
Morenish
424
Ardeonaig
Finglen Burn
Corrymuckloch
Achmore
Auchnafree
Creag Gharbh
2901
Creag Uchdag
2883
R Almond
2188
Meall Reamhar
Lochan Breaclaich
Loch Lednoch Resr
Ben Chonzie
3048
Auchnafree Hill
2589
2124
Meall Tarsuinn
Beich Burn
Spout Rolla
Invergeldie Burn
Glen Lednock
Invergeldie
Loch Turret Resr
Shaggie Burn
Sròn Mhór
2203
Glen Tarken
Loch Boltachan
R Lednock
Carn Chois
Glen Turret
Meall a'Mhadaidh
Falls of Keltie
Monzie
Dalveich
St Fillans
Hotel
Castle
LOCH EARN
Edinample
Ardvorlich
Ardtrostan
Dundurn
Dunira
Deil's Caldron
Lawers
Ochtertyre
Hosh
Comrie
Quoig
CRIEFF
Meall Reamhar
2225
Tullybannocher
Ross
Dalginross
R Earn
Lochlane
Ben Halton
2033
BEN VORLICH
3231
Allt Strath a Ghlinne
FOREST OF GLENARTNEY
Glen Artney
Water of Ruchill
Torlum
1291
Torlum Wood
Balloch
Culloch
Drummond Castle
Glen Ample
3189
Tighnablair
Dalchruin
Ochtermuthill
Muthill
Machany Water
2660
Beinn Each
1748
Ben Clach
2066
Meall Odhar
Findhu Glen
1172
Ardchullarie More
Coire Odhar
2072
Creag Beinn nan Eun
Glenlichorn
ROMAN FORTLET
ROAD

Map 20 — Loch Tay — Loch Earn

Reference	Estate Name
20a	FORESTRY COMMISSION
20b	CORRIE CARIE
20c	INNERHADDEN
20d	DALCHONSIE
20e	WEST TEMPAR
20f	CROSS MOUNT
20g	KYNACHAN
20h	GLENGOULANDIE
20i	GARTH
20k	GLENLYON
20j	NORTH CHESTHILL
20n	RORO
20o	INVERINAIN
20p	SOUTH CHESTHILL
20q	CULDAREMORE
20r	BEN LAWERS
20s	INCHGARTH
20t	AUCHNAFREE
20u	GLEN TURRET
20v	INVERGELDIE
20w	ARDVORLICH
20x	GLEN AMPLE
20y	GLEN ARTNEY
20z	INNERWICK
20za	GARROWS

Hills

Schiehallion
Carn Gorm
Carn Mairg Group
Ben Lawers Group
Farragon Hill
Meal Tairneachan
Meall nam Fuaran
Creag Uchdag
Ben Chonzie
Ben Vorlich
Stuc a' Chroin

Map/Estate Reference	Mountain or Mountain Group	Approaches	Estate	Contact	Remarks
20f	Schiehallion	Braes of Foss	*CROSSMOUNT Capt Ian de Sales La Terriere Dunalastair Pitlochry Perthshire	D. Dunlop Ballinloan Dunalastair Tel: Kinloch Rannoch (088 22) 305	Please use Forsetry Commission car park at Braes of Foss.
20g		From north-east	*KYNACHAN Col J.H. Horsfall DSO MC 3 Home Farm, Leek Wootton Warwick	Colonel V.A. Mavor Braes of Foss Farm Tummel Bridge, by Pitlochry Tel: Kenmore (088 73) 324	Car park is provided by monument.
20a			FORESTRY COMMISSION Portcullis House 21 India Street Glasgow G2 4PL	Perthshire Forest District Faskally, Pitlochry Perthshire Tel: Pitlochry (0796) 3437	
20h		From south and south-east	*GLENGOULANDIE H.S. & Mrs J.E. McAdam Glengoulandie, Foss by Pitlochry Perthshire	H.S. & Mrs J.E. McAdam Glengoulandie Foss Tel: Kenmore (088 73) 509	Parking in caravan site car park

* Members of East Glenlyon Deer Management Group

20i			*GARTH D.E.D. Johnson Brooklands House, Pipe Gate Market Drayton	H. McAdam Glengoulandie Tel: Kenmore (088 73) 509	
20s			*INCHGRATH E.D. Fry per Finlayson Hughes Estate Office, Aberfeldy Perthshire	Finlayson Hughes Estate Office Tel: Aberfeldy (0887) 20904	
20k			*GLENLYON T.R.M. Ashfield Sevington Manor, Tichbourne Arlesford Hants	D.T. Kerr Glenlyon House Fortingall, Aberfeldy Tel: Kenmore (088 73) 313	Track up Glen Mullin behind Glen Lyon House.
20a	Carn Gorm Carn Mairg Group	From north-west	FORESTRY COMMISSION Portcullis House 21 India Street Glasgow G2 4PL	Perthshire Forest District Faskally, Pitlochry Perthshire Tel: Pitlochry (0796) 3437	
20b			*CORRIE CARIE M.D. Pearson The Barracks Kinloch Rannoch	Head Keeper Tel: Bridge of Gaur (088 23) 248	

*Member of East Glenlyon Deer Management Group

Map/Estate Reference	Mountain or Mountain Group	Approaches	Estate	Contact	Remarks
20c		From north	*INNERHADDEN L. Barclay Innerhadden, Kinloch Rannoch	L. Barclay Tel: Kinloch Rannoch (088 22) 344	
20d			*DALCHONSIE Col J.H. Horsfall DSO MC 3 Home Farm, Leek Wootton Warwick	Colonel V.A. Mavor Braes of Foss Farm Tummel Bridge by Pitlochry Tel: Kenmore (088 73) 324	Car park is provided by monument
20e			*WEST TEMPAR J. Hepburn Wright The Farmhouse, West Tempar Kinloch Rannoch	J. Hepburn Wright Tel: Kinloch Rannoch (088 22) 317	
20f		From north-east	*CROSSMOUNT Capt Ian de Sales La Terriere Dunalastair, Pitlochry Perthshire	D. Dunlop Ballinloan, Dunalastair Tel: Kinloch Rannoch (088 22) 305	
20z		Innerwick	INNERWICK Mr & Mrs R. Whewell Innerwick, Glenlyon Aberfeldy Perthshire	J.T. Boscawen& Partners Boltachan House By Aberfeldy Tel: Aberfeldy (0887) 20496	

*Member of the East Glenlyon Deer Management Group

20m		From south	*NORTH CHESTHILL Trustees of Mrs I.K. Molteno Dr M.J. Riddell Dornoch Lodge, Glenlyon Aberfeldy	The Stalker Tel: Glenlyon (088 77) 207	
20a			FORESTRY COMMISSION Portcullis House 21 India Street Glasgow G2 4PI	Perthshire Forest District Faskally, Pitlochry Perthshire Tel: Pitlochry (0796) 3437	
20k		From south-east	*GLENLYON T.R.M. Ashfield Sevington Manor, Tichborne, Arlesford Hants	D.T. KERR Glenlyon House Fortingall, Aberfeldy Tel: Kenmore (088 73) 313	Track up Glen Mullin behind Glen Lyon House.
20n	Ben Lawers Group	From north	*RORO H. Hargrave Roroyere Glenlyon	D. Campbell Tel: Bridge of Balgie (088 76) 216	
20o			*INVERINAIN J.L. Curtis per Finlayson Hughes Estate Office, Aberfeldy Perthshire	H. Shearer Tel: Glenlyon (088 77) 233	

* Member of East Glenlyon Deer Management Group

Map/Estate Reference	Mountain or Mountain Group	Approaches	Estate	Contact	Remarks
20p			*SOUTH CHESTHILL Maj Gen Ramsay per Strutt & Parker 26 Walker Street, Edinburgh	H. Shearer Tel: Glenlyon (088 77) 233	
20q			*CULDAREMORE Mr Common Culdaremore, Glenlyon	Mr Common Tel: Kenmore (088 73) 364	
20a		From east	FORESTRY COMMISSION Portcullis House 21 India Street Glasgow G2 4PL	Perthshire Forest District Faskally, Pitlochry Perthshire Tel: Pitlochry (0796) 3437	
20r		From south	BEN LAWERS National Trust for Scotland 5 Charlotte Square Edinburgh	The Ranger Fagus, Manse Road Killin Tel: Killin (056 72) 248 or 397	Please take care to avoid damage to plants in the high corries and wet flushes.
20u	Ben Chonzie	Glen Turret	GLEN TURRET Glen Turret Estates Ltd Glen Turret, Crieff Perthshire PH7 4LD	Tel: Crieff (0764) 2927	

*Member of East Glen Lyon Deer Management Group

20v		Glen Lednock	INVERGELDIE James S. Priestley Upton Manor, Upton Nr Andover, Hants. SP11	Tel: Comrie (0764) 619 or 240
20t		From north	AUCHNAFREE Major Sir James Whitaker Amulree,Dunkeld Perthshire PH8 0EH	
20t	Meall nam Fuaran	From south	AUCHNAFREE (as above)	
20za		From north	GARROWS Mrs P.P. Kemp-Welch Garrows Estate, Amulree Dunkeld, Perthshire PH8 0DE	
20a	Creag Uchdag	Loch Tay	FORESTRY COMMISSION Portcullis House 21 India Street Glasgow G2 4PL	Perthshire Forest District Faskally, Pitlochry Perthshire Tel: Pitlochry (0796) 3437
20w	Ben Vorlich Stuc a'Chroin	Ardvorlich	ARDVORLICH Mr Alexander Donald Stewart Ardvorlich, Lochearnhead Perthshire SK19 8QE	Estate Keeper Findoglen, St. Fillans Perthshire Tel: St. Fillans (076 485) 260

Map/Estate Reference	Mountain or Mountain Group	Approaches	Estate	Contact	Remarks
20x		Glen Ample	GLEN AMPLE	Tel: Lochearnhead (056 73) 202	
20y			GLEN ARTNEY	Tel: Muthill (076 481) 257	

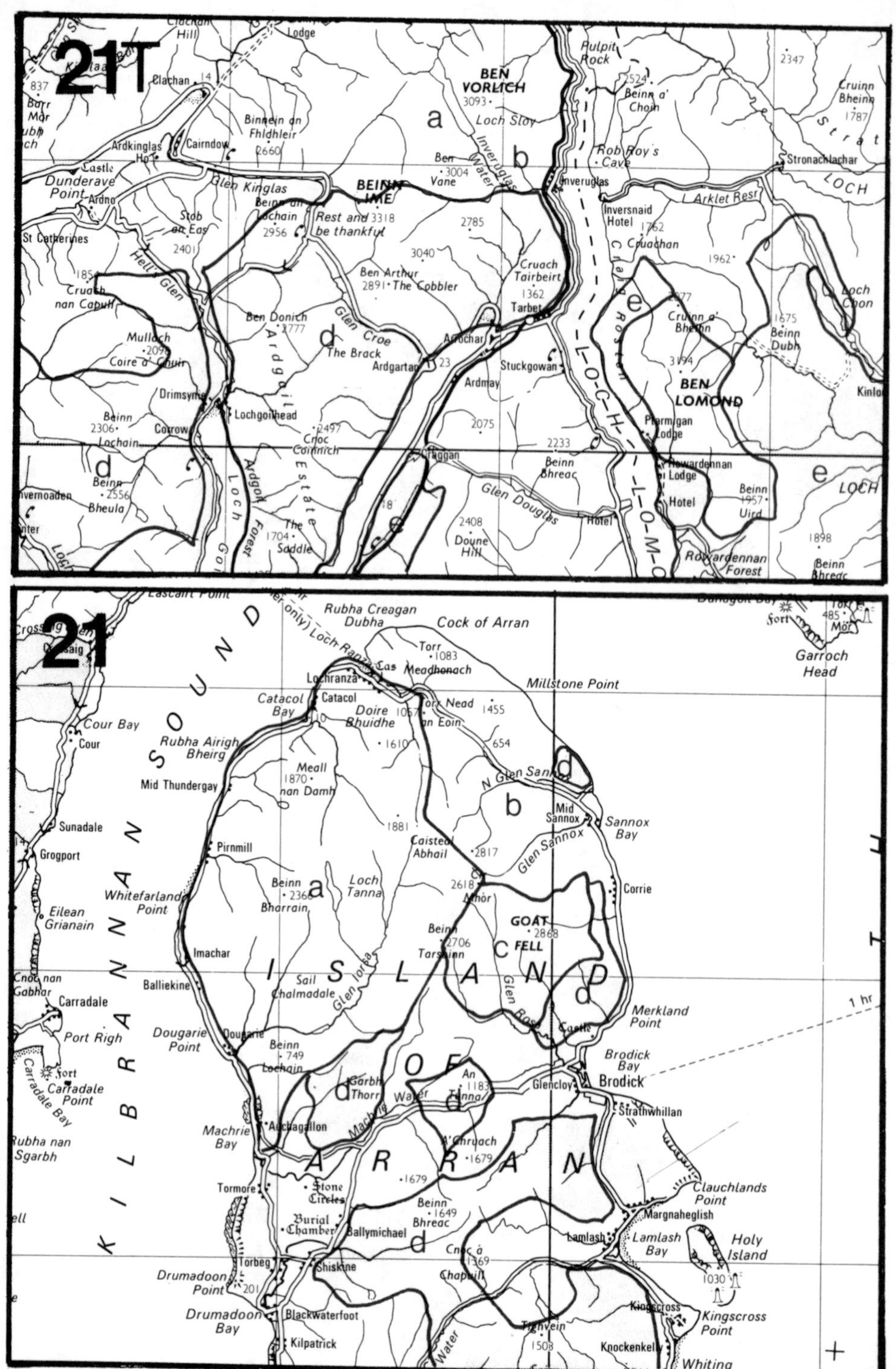

21T
BEN VORLICH
3093
Loch Sloy
Inveruglas Water
Ben Vane
3004
BEINN IME
3318
Beinn an Lochain
2956
Rest and be thankful
Binnein an Fhidhleir
2660
Clachan
Cairndow
Ardkinglas Ho
Castle
Dunderave Point
Ardno
Glen Kinglas
Stob an Eas
2401
St Catherines
Hell's Glen
1854
Cruach nan Capull
Mullach
2096
Coire a' Chuir
Drimsynie
Lochgoilhead
Beinn Lochain
2306
Corrow
Beinn Bheula
2556
Invernoaden
Ardgoil Forest
Loch Goil
Ben Donich
2777
Ardgoil
Glen Croe
The Brack
Ardgartan
23
Arrochar
Ben Arthur
2891
The Cobbler
3040
2785
Cruach Tairbeirt
1362
Tarbet
Cnoc Coinnich
2497
Ardgoil Estate
The Saddle
1704
Ardmay
Stuckgowan
2075
2233
Beinn Bhreac
Glen Douglas
2408
Doune Hill
Hotel
Pulpit Rock
2524
Beinn a' Choin
Rob Roy's Cave
Inveruglas
Inversnaid Hotel
1762
Cruachan
Arklet Resr
Stronachlachar
LOCH
2347
Cruinn Bheinn
1787
Craig Rostan
1962
2077
Cruinn a' Bheinn
3194
BEN LOMOND
Ptarmigan Lodge
Rowardennan Lodge
Hotel
Beinn Uird
1957
Loch Chon
1675
Beinn Dubh
Rowardennan Forest
1898
Beinn Bhreac
LOCH LOMOND
a
b
d
e
21
Rubha Creagan Dubha
Cock of Arran
Loch Ranza
Torr Meadhonach
1083
Lochranza
Catacol Bay
Catacol
Doire Bhuidhe
Torr Nead an Eoin
1057
1455
Millstone Point
1610
654
N Glen Sannox
Mid Sannox
Sannox Bay
Meall nan Damh
1870
1881
Caisteal Abhail
2817
Glen Sannox
Corrie
Cour Bay
Cour
Rubha Airigh Bheirg
Mid Thundergay
Sunadale
Grogport
Pirnmill
Whitefarland Point
Eilean Grianain
Beinn Bharrain
2368
Loch Tanna
2618
Am Mhor
GOAT FELL
2868
Beinn Tarsuinn
2706
Imachar
Balliekine
Cnoc nan Gabhar
Carradale
Port Righ
Fort
Carradale Point
Carradale Bay
Sail Chalmadale
Glen Iorsa
Glen Rosa
Castle
Merkland Point
ISLAND OF ARRAN
KILBRANNAN SOUND
Dougarie Point
Dougarie
Beinn Lochain
749
Garbh Thorr
An Tunna
1183
Machrie Water
Glencloy
Brodick Bay
Brodick
Strathwhillan
1 hr
Machrie Bay
Auchagallon
A' Chruach
1679
Rubha nan Sgarbh
Tormore
Stone Circles
Burial Chamber
Ballymichael
Beinn Bhreac
1649
Clauchlands Point
Margnaheglish
Lamlash
Lamlash Bay
Holy Island
1030
Drumadoon Point
Torbeg
Shiskine
201
Cnoc a Chapuill
1369
Drumadoon Bay
Blackwaterfoot
Kilpatrick
Tighvein
1503
Kingscross
Kingscross Point
Knockenkelly
Whiting
Garroch Head
Fort
485
Mor
a
b
c
d

Map 21T — Arrochar — Ben Lomond

Reference	Estate Name
21T/a	SLOY
21T/b	INVERUGLAS
21T/d	ARGYLL FOREST PARK
21T/e	FORESTRY COMMISSION
21T/f	BEN LOMOND

Hills

Arrochar Alps
Beinn Ime
The Cobbler
Ben Lomond Group
Cowal
Ben Donich
The Brack
Ben Vorlich

Map 21B — Arran

Reference	Estate Name
21B/a	DOUGARIE
21B/b	SANNOX
21B/c	GOATFELL & GLEN ROSA
21B/d	FORESTRY COMMISSION
21B/e	

Hills

Glen Sannox
Beinn Bharrain
Caisteal Abhail
Goatfell
Cir Mhor
Glen Rosa
Beinn Tarsuinn
Beinn Bhreac

Map/Estate Reference	Mountain or Mountain Group	Approaches	Estate	Contact	Remarks
21T/d	Ben Vorlich Arrochar Alps (Beinn Ime The Cobbler) Cowal	Loch Long side and Rest and be Thankful	ARGYLL FOREST PARK FORESTRY COMMISSION Portcullis House 21 India Street Glasgow G2 4PL	Cowal Forest District Kilmun, by Dunoon Argyll Tel: Dunoon (0364) 98666 or Ardgartan Office, Arrochar Tel: Arrochar (030 12) 597	
21T/a		Inveruglas and Ardlui	SLOY North of Scotland Hydro ELectric Board	Tel: Inveruglas (030 14) 245	Do not park cars at the entrance to the Loch Sloy road.
21T/b			INVERUGLAS		
21T/c	Ben Donich The Brack	Loch Long, Glen Croe, Rest and be Thankful	ARGYLL FOREST PARK FORESTRY COMMISSION Portcullis House 21 India Street Glasgow G2 4PL	Cowal Forest District Kilmun, by Dunoon Argyll Tel: Dunoon (0364) 98666	
21T/f	Ben Lomond Group	Rowardennan	BEN LOMOND National Trust for Scotland 5 Charlotte Square Edinburgh	The Factor (West) National Trust for Scotland Hutcheson's Hall, 158 Ingram St.. Glasgow Tel: 041 552 8391	

21T/e		Lower slopes	FORESTRY COMMISSION (as above)		
21B/b	Glen Sannox	From north	SANNOX		
21B/c		From south	GOATFELL & GLENROSA National Trust for Scotland 5 Charlotte Square Edinburgh	The Ranger Brodick Castle Tel: Brodick (0770) 2202	Car park at Brodick Castle.
21B/a		From west	DOUGARIE The Estate Office, Dougarie Isle of Arran KA27 8EB	Head Stalker The Towers, Dougarie Tel: Machrie (077 084) 224	
21B/a	Beinn Bharrain Caisteal Abhail	All routes	DOUGARIE (as above)	Head Stalker (as above)	
21B/c	Goatfell Cir Mhor A'Chir	Glen Rosa	GOATFELL & GLENROSA (as above)	The Ranger (as above)	
21B/d	Glen Rosa Beinn Tarsuinn		FORESTRY COMMISSION Portcullis House 21 India Street Glasgow G2 4PL	Cowal Forest District Kilmun, by Dunoon Argyll Tel: Dunoon (0369) 84666	

Map/Estate Reference	Mountain or Mountain Group	Approaches	Estate	Contact	Remarks
21B/a		From west	DOUGARIE (as above)	Head Stalker (as above)	
21B/b		From north	SANNOX (as above)		
21B/a	Beinn Bhreac	North and south	FORESTRY COMMISSION Portcullis 21 India Street Glasgow G2 4PL	Cowal Forest District Kilmun, by Dunoon Argyll Tel Dunoon (0369) 84666	

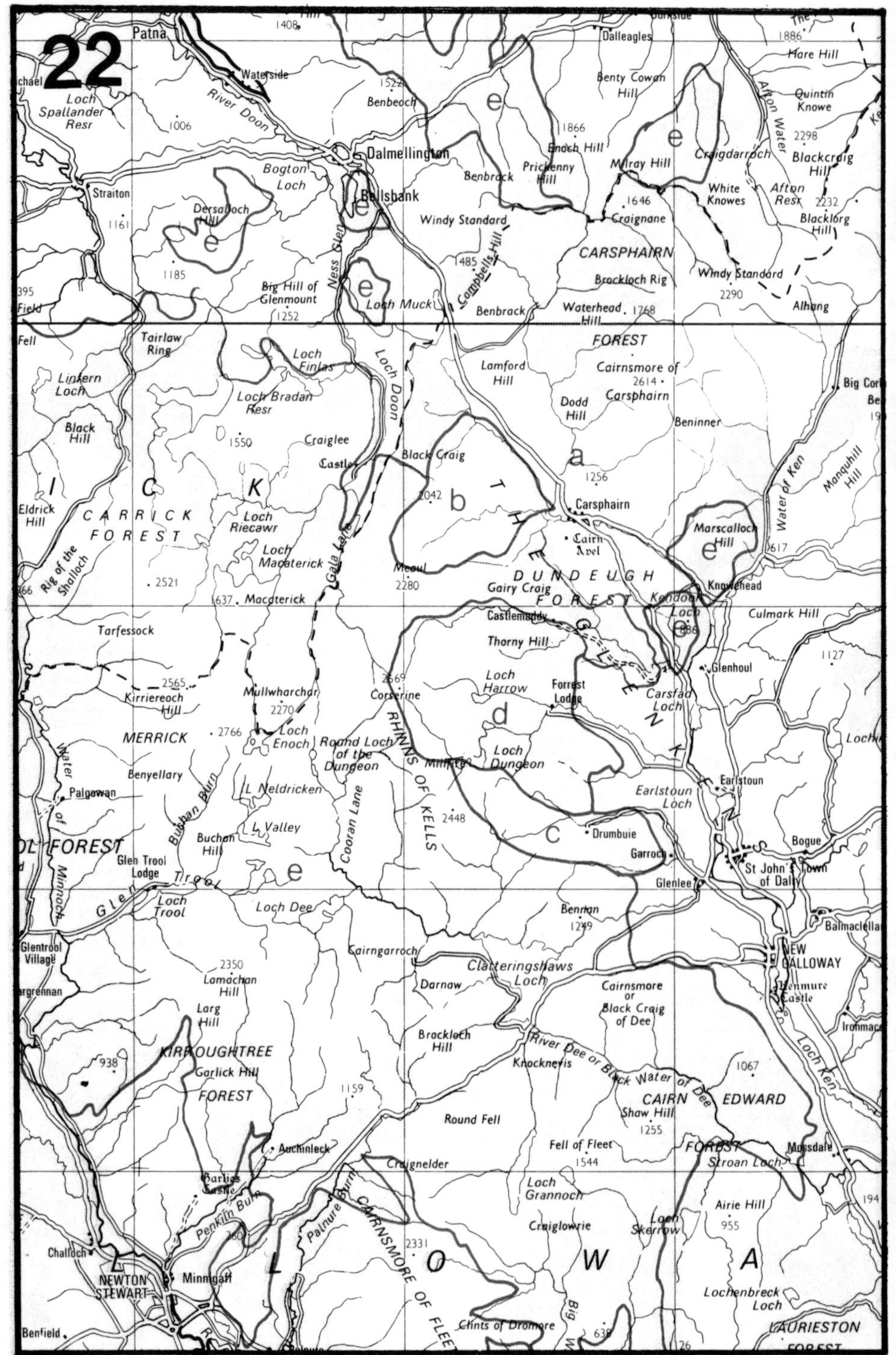

22
Patna
Waterside
River Doon
Loch Spallander Resr
1408
1522
Benbeoch
1006
Dalmellington
Bellshank
Bogton Loch
Straiton
Dersalloch Hill
1161
1185
Big Hill of Glenmount
1252
Ness Glen
Loch Muck
Dalleagles
Benty Cowan Hill
1866
Enoch Hill
Prickenny Hill
Benbrack
Windy Standard
Campbells Hill
1485
Benbrack
Milray Hill
1646
Craignane
CARSPHAIRN
Brockloch Rig
Waterhead Hill
1768
1886
Hare Hill
Quintin Knowe
Afton Water
Craigdarroch
2298
Blackcraig Hill
White Knowes
Afton Resr
2232
Blacklorg Hill
Windy Standard
2290
Alhang
Tairlaw Ring
Linfern Loch
Black Hill
Loch Finlas
Loch Bradan Resr
1550
Craiglee
Castle
Loch Doon
Black Craig
2042
Lamford Hill
FOREST
Cairnsmore of Carsphairn
2614
Dodd Hill
Beninner
1256
Carsphairn
Cairn Avel
Big Corl
Water of Ken
Manquhill Hill
Marscalloch Hill
617
Eldrick Hill
CARRICK FOREST
Rig of the Shalloch
Loch Riecawr
Loch Macaterick
Gala Lane
Meaul
2280
2521
1637
Macaterick
THE GLENKENS
DUNDEUGH FOREST
Gairy Craig
Kendoon Loch
Knowehead
Castlemaddy
Thorny Hill
Culmark Hill
1127
Glenhoul
Tarfessock
2565
Kirriereoch Hill
Mullwharchar
2270
2669
Corserine
Loch Harrow
Forrest Lodge
Carsfad Loch
MERRICK
2766
Loch Enoch
Round Loch of the Dungeon
RHINNS OF KELLS
Millfire
Loch Dungeon
Water of Minnoch
Benyellary
Palgowan
L Neldricken
Cooran Lane
2448
Earlstoun Loch
Earlstoun
Buchan Burn
L Valley
Buchan Hill
Drumbuie
Garroch
Bogue
St John's Town of Dalry
FOREST
Glen Trool Lodge
Glen Trool
Loch Trool
Loch Dee
Glenlee
Bennan
1249
Balmaclellan
Glentrool Village
Cairngarroch
Clatteringshaws Loch
NEW GALLOWAY
Kenmure Castle
2350
Lamachan Hill
Darnaw
Cairnsmore or Black Craig of Dee
Larg Hill
Brockloch Hill
River Dee or Black Water of Dee
Knocknevis
Ironmacannie
Loch Ken
1067
938
KIRROUGHTREE
Garlick Hill
FOREST
1159
CAIRN EDWARD
Shaw Hill
1255
Round Fell
Auchinleck
Craignelder
Fell of Fleet
1544
FOREST
Stroan Loch
Mossdale
Barclye Castle
Penkiln Burn
Palnure Burn
CAIRNSMORE OF FLEET
Loch Grannoch
Craiglowrie
Loch Skerrow
Airie Hill
955
2331
Challoch
NEWTON STEWART
Minnigaff
G A L L O W A
Lochenbreck Loch
Benfield
Clints of Dromore
Big Water
638
LAURIESTON FOREST

Map 22 — Galloway Hills

Reference	Estate Name
22a	HOLM OF DALTALLOCHAN
22b	DRUMGRANGE
22c	GARROCH
22d	FORREST ESTATE
22e	GALLOWAY FOREST PARK

Hills

Cairnsmore of Carsphairn
Rhinns of Kells
Merrick
Glentrool Hills
Cairnsmore of Fleet

Map/Estate Reference	Mountain or Mountain Group	Approaches	Estate	Contact	Remarks
22a	Cairnsmore of Carsphairn	From Bridgend Cottage on A713 3/4 mile north of Carsphairn Village	HOLM OF DALTALLOCHAN C.W. Campbell Holm of Daltallochan, Carsphairn Castle Douglas.	C. W. Campbell Tel: Carsphairn (064 46) 208	
22b	Rhinns of Kells	Garryhorn area	DRUMGRANGE Trustees of the late A.R. Cathcart per Elvy & Company Bannerbank, Newton Mearns Glasgow	D. Wallace Garryhorn	Please call at steading. Use gates as fences are electrified.
22c		Rig of Clenrie	GARROCH Mr & Mrs R. Roper-Caldbeck Garroch New Galloway Castle Douglas	Mr & Mrs R. Roper-Caldbeck Tel: Dalry (064 43) 205	The Southern Upland Way crosses the estate over Drumbuie and Clenrie Farms.
22d		Garroch Glen	FORREST ESTATE Fred Olsen Ltd Forrest Estate Dalry Castle Douglas	Fred Olsen Ltd Forrest Estate Tel: Dalry (064 43) 230	Please use car parks provided.

22e		Craigencallie GR 503 779	GALLOWAY FOREST PARK Forestry Commission 231 Corstorphine Rd Edinburgh	Forest District Office Creebridge, Newton Stewart Tel: Newton Stewart (0671) 3285	Park at Craigencallie.
22e	Merrick and Glentrool Hills	All routes	GALLOWAY FOREST PARK Forestry Commission 231 Corstorphine Road Edinburgh	Forest District Office Creebridge, Newton Stewart Tel: Newton Stewart (0671) 3285	Camping at Caldons.
22e	Cairnsmore of Fleet	Craignelder, Craigronald Deer Park on A712 GR 523 732	GALLOWAY FOREST PARK (as above)	Forest District Office (as above)	Parking at Craigencallie.

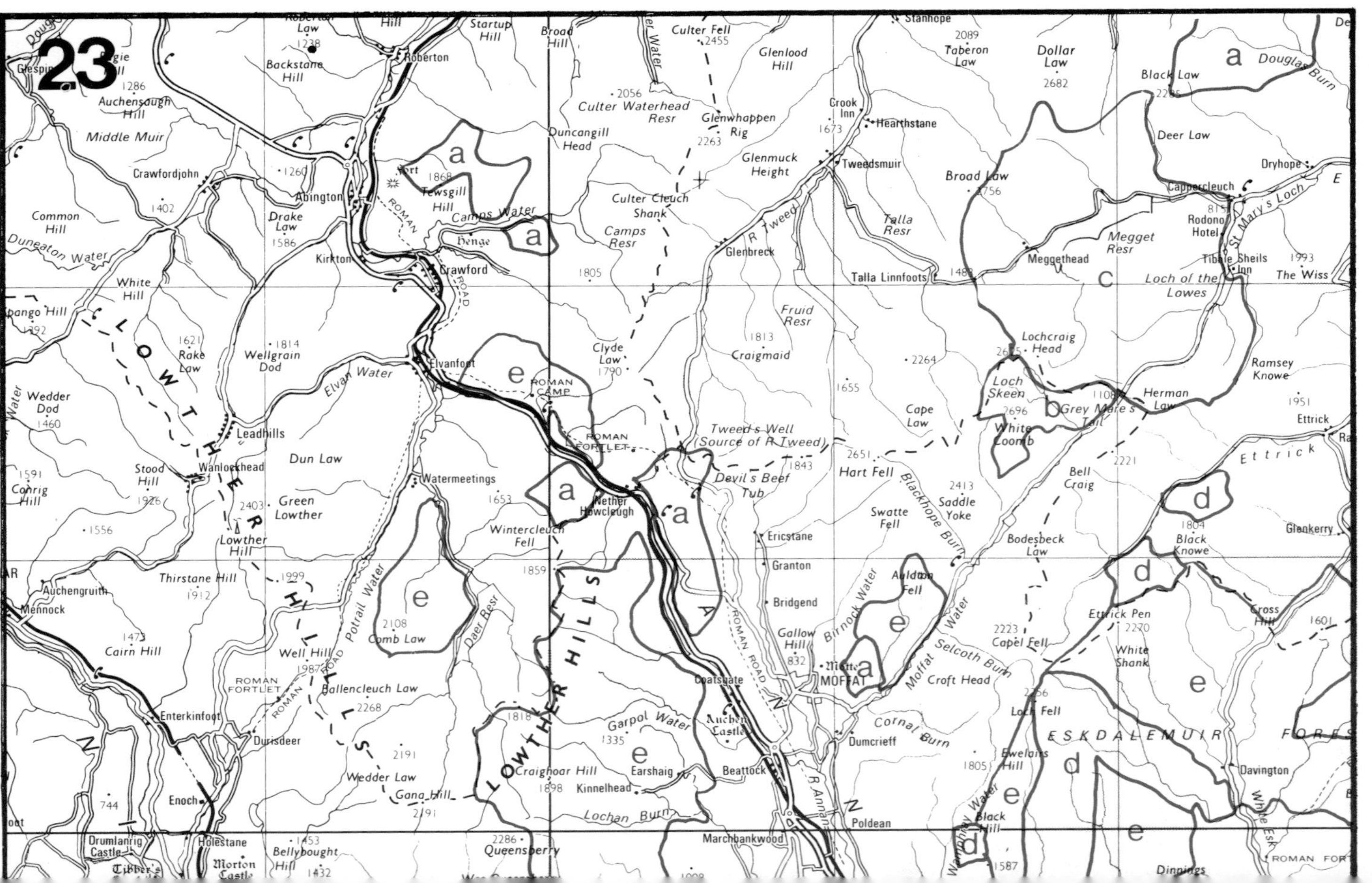
23
Glespin
Auchensaugh Hill
Middle Muir
Crawfordjohn
Common Hill
Duneaton Water
White Hill
Backstane Hill
Roberton
Startup Hill
Broad Hill
Culter Fell
Glenlood Hill
Culter Waterhead Resr
Glenwhappen Rig
Duncangill Head
Glenmuck Height
Crook Inn
Hearthstane
Tweedsmuir
Stanhope
Taberon Law
Dollar Law
Black Law
Douglas Burn
Deer Law
Dryhope
Cappercleuch
Rodono Hotel
St Mary's Loch
Broad Law
Abington
Drake Law
Tewsgill Hill
Camps Water
Henge
Kirkton
Crawford
ROMAN ROAD
Culter Cleuch Shank
Camps Resr
R Tweed
Glenbreck
Talla Resr
Talla Linnfoots
Meggethead
Megget Resr
Tibbie Sheils Inn
The Wiss
Loch of the Lowes
Rake Law
Wellgrain Dod
Elvanfoot
Elvan Water
ROMAN CAMP
Clyde Law
Fruid Resr
Craigmaid
Lochcraig Head
Loch Skeen
White Coomb
Grey Mare's Tail
Herman Law
Ramsey Knowe
Ettrick
Wedder Dod
Leadhills
Dun Law
ROMAN FORTLET
Tweed's Well (Source of R Tweed)
Cape Law
Hart Fell
Blackhope Burn
Saddle Yoke
Bell Craig
Ettrick
Stood Hill
Wanlockhead
Watermeetings
Devil's Beef Tub
Swatte Fell
Green Lowther
Wether Hawcleugh
Wintercleuch Fell
Ericstane
Bodesbeck Law
Black Knowe
Glenkerry
Carrig Hill
Lowther Hill
Granton
Bridgend
Auldton Fell
Birnock Water
Thirstane Hill
Auchengruith
Mennock
Potrail Water
Daer Resr
LOWTHER HILLS
Comb Law
Moffat Water
Ettrick Pen
Cross Hill
Cairn Hill
Well Hill
Gallow Hill
MOFFAT
Capel Fell
White Shank
Selcoth Burn
Croft Head
Coatsgate
Ballencleuch Law
Enterkinfoot
Garpol Water
Auchen Castle
Cornal Burn
Loch Fell
ESKDALEMUIR
Durisdeer
Dumcrieff
Craighoar Hill
Earshaig
Beattock
Ewelairs Hill
Davington
Wedder Law
Kinnelhead
R Annan
Enoch
Gana Hill
Lochan Burn
Poldean
Wamphray Water
Black Hill
White Esk
Drumlanrig Castle
Holestane
Bellybought Hill
Morton Castle
Queensberry
Marchbankwood
Dinnings
ROMAN FORT

Map 23 — Moffat Hills

Reference	Estate Name
23a	ECONOMIC FORESTRY (1)
23b	GREY MARE'S TAIL, WHITE COOMBE & LOCH SKEEN
23c	WEMYSS & MARCH ESTATE
23d	ECONOMIC FORESTRY (2)
23e	FORESTRY COMMISSION

Hills

Hart Fell
White Coombe
Ettrick Hills
Eskdalemuir Forest
Lowther Hills

Map/Estate Reference	Mountain or Mountain Group	Approaches	Estate	Contact	Remarks
23a	Hart Fell White Coombe	Birnock Water	ECONOMIC FORESTRY LTD Forestry House, Moffat Dumfries-shire	The Manager Tel: Hawick (0450) 78353	Please use contact number in times of high fire risk.
23b		Loch Skeen	GREY MARE'S TAIL, WHITE COOMBE & LOCH SKEEN National Trust for Scotland 5 Charlotte Square Edinburgh	Chief Ranger National Trust for Scotland 5 Charlotte Square Edinburgh Tel: 031 226 5922	Seasonal Ranger in July/August only.
23c			WEMYSS & MARCH ESTATE Lord Wemyss Trust Estate Office Longniddry East Lothian	Norman Douglas Farm Manager Catslackburn, Yarrow Tel: Yarrow (0750) 8206	Leave cars at Winterhope Burn at shepherd's house.
23c	Ettrick Hills	Riskinhope,Ettrick	WEMYSS & MARCH ESTATE (as above)	Estate Office Tel: Aberlady (087 57) 201	This route is part of the Southern Upland Way.
23d	Eskdalemuir Forest		ECONOMIC FORESTRY LTD 1 Northbridge Street, Hawick Roxburghshire	Estate Office Tel: Hawick (0450) 78353	

23e			FORESTRY COMMISSION 55/57 Moffat Road Dumfries DG1 1NP	Forest District Office Lockerbie Tel: Lockerbie (057 62) 2858
23e	Lowther Hills	A74	FORESTRY COMMISSION (as above)	(as above)

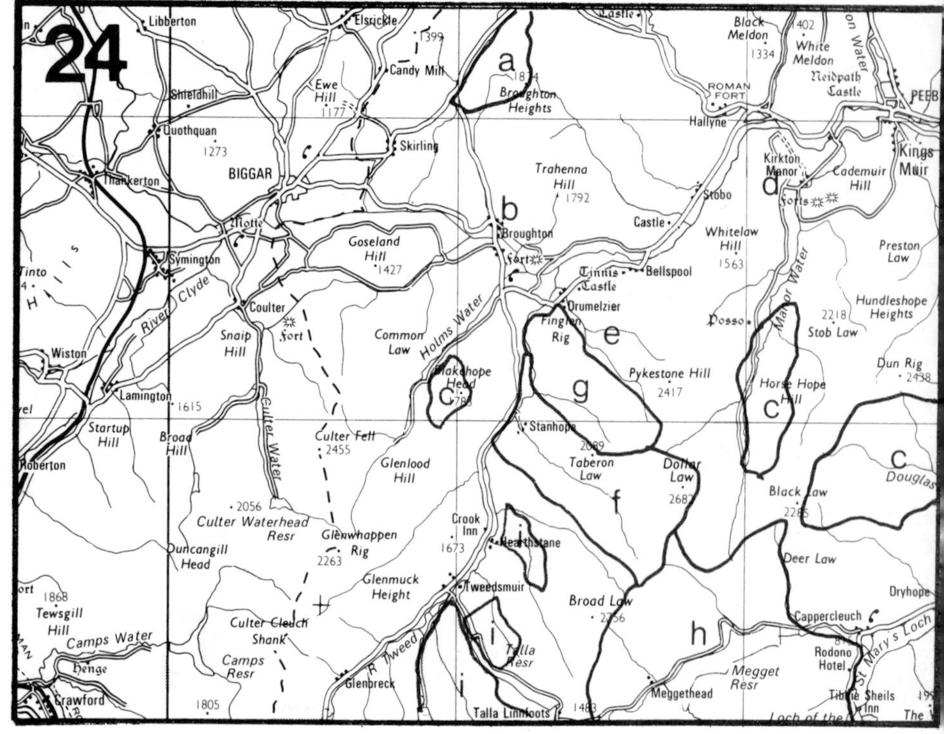

24
Libberton
Elsrickle
1399
Candy Mill
a
Broughton Heights
Black Meldon
1334
1402
White Meldon
Neidpath Castle
ROMAN FORT
Hallyne
Shieldhill
Ewe Hill
1177
Quothquan
1273
Skirling
Thankerton
BIGGAR
Trahenna Hill
1792
Kirkton Manor
Cademuir Hill
Kings Muir
Stobo
d
Forts
b
Motte
Broughton
Castle
Whitelaw Hill
1563
Preston Law
Goseland Hill
1427
Symington
Fort
Tinnis Castle
Bellspool
Tinto
River Clyde
Coulter
Drumelzier
Snaip Hill
Fort
Common Law
Holms Water
e
Posso
Manor Water
2218
Stob Law
Hundleshope Heights
Dun Rig
2438
Wiston
Blakehope Head
c
Pykestone Hill
2417
g
Horse Hope Hill
c
Lamington
1615
Culter Water
Stanhope
2089
Startup Hill
Broad Hill
Culter Fell
2455
Taberon Law
Dollar Law
2682
c
Douglas
Roberton
Glenlood Hill
f
Black Law
2285
2056
Culter Waterhead Resr
Crook Inn
1673
Glenwhappen Rig
2263
Hearthstane
Duncangill Head
Deer Law
Glenmuck Height
Tweedsmuir
1868
Tewsgill Hill
Dryhope
Broad Law
Camps Water
Culter Cleuch Shank
Cappercleuch
h
Talla Resr
Rodono Hotel
Henge
Camps Resr
R Tweed
Megget Resr
St Mary's Loch
Glenbreck
Crawford
Meggethead
Tibbie Sheils Inn
1805
Talla Linnfoots
i

Map 24 — Broad Law

Reference	Estate Name
24a	LOCHURD
24b	STIRKFIELD
24c	ECONOMIC FORESTRY LTD
24d	CASTLEHILL
24e	DRUMELZIER PLACE
24f	STANHOPE
24g	DAWYCK ESTATES
24h	WEMYSS & MARCH ESTATE
24i	FORESTRY COMMISSION

Hills

Broughton Heights
Culter Hills
Manor Valley
Dollar Law
Black Law
Broad Law
Cramalt Craig

Map/Estate Reference	Mountain or Mountain Group	Approaches	Estate	Contact	Remarks
24a	Broughton Heights	Lochurd Farm	LOCHURD W.A.B. Noble Lochurd, West Linton Peebles-shire	W.A.B. Noble Lochurd Tel: Skirling (089 96) 244	Fences are either all electrified or have electric scare wires, so please use gates and close them behind you.
24b			STIRKFIELD M. Hamilton Corstane, Broughton Biggar	M. Hamilton Tel: Broughton (089 94) 203	Electric fences in operation.
24c	Culter Hills	Blakehope Head Glenlood Hill	ECONOMIC FORESTRY LTD 1 Northbridge Street Hawick Roxburghshire	The Manager Estate Office Tel: Hawick (0450) 78353	
24d	Manor Valley	Track up Canada Hill	CASTLEHILL J.R. Nash Castlehill Farm Kirkton Manor Pebbles-shire	J.R. Nash Tel: Kirkton Manor (072 14) 218	

24e		Drumelzier Law	DRUMELZIER PLACE Mrs S. Luka's Trust c/o M. Luka Drumelzier Place Broughton	M. Luka Drumelzier Place Tel: Broughton (089 94) 238	
24c		Dun Rig Deuchar Law	ECONOMIC FORESTRY (as above)	(as above)	
24f	Dollar Law	Stanhope Burn	STANHOPE A.F.R.C. Stanhope Farm Broughton ML12 6QT	Farm Manager Stanhope Tel: Tweedsmuir (089 97) 276	Electric fences in operation.
24g		Low Hills - Scrape	DAWYCK ESTATES Col. A.N. Balfour Dawyck House Stobo	J. Hunter Dawyck Mill Tel: Stobo (072 16) 217	
24h	Black Law	Redside Head Black Law Deer Law Milehope Head Henderland Hill Cappercleuch	WEMYSS & MARCH ESTATE Lord Wemyss Trust Estate Office Longniddry East Lothian	J. Mitchell Tel: Cappercleuch (0750) 4244	

Map/Estate Reference	Mountain or Mountain Group	Approaches	Estate	Contact	Remarks
24h	Broad Law Cramalt Craig	From south	WEMYSS & MARCH ESTATE Lord Wemyss Trust Estate Office Longniddry East Lothian	Norman Douglas Catslackburn, Yarrow Tel: Yarrow (0750) 8206 or Shepherd (0750) 4236	Leave cars at Meggethead.
24f		From north	STANHOPE (as above)	Farm Manager (as above)	
24i		From Tweedsmuir	FORESTRY COMMISSION 55/57 Moffat Road Dumfries DG1 1NP	Forest District Office Greenside, Peebles Tel: Peebles (0721) 20448/20218	

INDEX OF MOUNTAINS AND OTHER AREAS REFERRED TO IN TEXT